On Active Service Series.

THREE CHEVRONS

THREE CHEVRONS
BY "OREX"
(MAJOR H. F. BIDDER, D.S.O.)

LONDON: JOHN LANE THE BODLEY HEAD
NEW YORK: JOHN LANE COMPANY MCMXIX

DEDICATED TO

THE YOUNG MEN WHO HAVE FALLEN
IN THE WAR

TWENTY-TWO

Twenty-two
At the end of the week, if he'd seen it through.
We left his grave in the curé's hands :
    I met him as I was coming away,
A white-haired man in cassock and bands,
    And I showed him where it lay.

" Twenty-two—
Yet he's older than you or I, m'sieu,
And the riddle of Time for him is read.
    Yes, I will see the grave kept trim,
And after the prayers for our own are said
    I will add a prayer for him."

Twenty-two—
Some one will bitterly weep for you,
Yet she'll lift her head with a wonderful pride.
    " He was my son, and his life he gave.
Shall I grudge such a gift, though my heart has died ?
    He was brave ; I must be brave."

Twenty-two—
Ah, for the dreams that will never come true !
All that the world should have held in store.
    You were willing to die, though you loved to live.
We must be ready to follow, the more
    That we've many years less to give.

FOREWORD

Publishers, as a rule, look askance at
letters; for they know, by experience, how
rare it is to come across private correspondence that has either value or interest for any
other circle than that of the correspondents'
own immediate acquaintance.

Written to relatives or friends, who read
them with the eye of affection and the in-
sight of a common understanding, such
private letters may be intensely engrossing
to their recipients. But take them out of
their particular setting: expose them, in
the cold light of print, to the eye of a public
that reads only the written lines, not having
the clues for reading between them—in
ninety-nine cases out of a hundred all the
interest goes, all the charm evaporates.
Their private virtues become, so to speak,
public vices. The very qualities that made
them so delightful as intimate communica-

tions is fatal to them when collected into a printed book.

In the hundredth case, however, one is fortunate enough to run up against the blessed exception and to find a correspondent whose private letters to his friends have that intrinsic and independent value which can face the searching test of the printed page.

It is so (unless the writer of this foreword is deceived) with the collection of letters contained in the present volume. They were written originally by an officer of the British Army to relatives or friends, describing and commenting on his experiences as they occurred, without any thought of his remarks ever going beyond the family circle. But copies of the letters had been kept for him as interesting memoranda for his future reference ; and, quite by chance, he showed some of them one day to the writer of this foreword. The latter, expecting to be rather bored by the perusal of the gallant officer's correspondence with other people, had the agreeable surprise of finding himself a good deal interested and entertained instead. And the outcome of it was that he persuaded the officer to let him submit the letters to Mr. John Lane, who, on his reader's report, at once accepted them.

It was the officer's express stipulation that his letters, if published, should be issued exactly as they stood (subject to certain necessary excisions), and not in any way written up for the sake of effect. Not that he supposed them incapable of improvement in that direction, but he felt it would hardly be playing the game. It only remains to say that this stipulation has been strictly observed.

R. M. F.

THREE CHEVRONS

THREE CHEVRONS

LETTER 1

The Depot,
5th August, 1914.

I got down last night after journeying through one of the most perfect evenings I have ever seen. The low sun lit up the woods and the cornfields, and the marshes with their cattle, and the villages. It had sunk when we passed the city ; the castle and church and town below were blue under a flaming sky. It was all very beautiful— and seemed very well worth fighting for.

To-day has been an inspiring day —officers and men coming in at intervals. The men come in in very good form —very cheery, and inspired by an extraordinary depth of feeling against Germany. The general feeling, I believe, is one of relief : Germany is felt to have been a challenge to us for so

long. " You've threatened us all this time ;
all right, let's see who *is* the better man "
seems to be the underlying idea.   One man
sat crying on the seat by the Guard Room
because the Doctor rejected him. " I've been
doing navvy's work," he said, " and I'm
good enough for that."

The men arrive quiet and respectable for
the most part—I am now talking of regular
Reservists : the Special Reservists are em-
bodied on Friday.   They are a *very* useful
looking lot, and greet the officers in a very
friendly spirit.

As they gather round the Mobilization
Store, old pals recognize each other and
most cheery meetings take place.

To-night the first draft went away to the
2nd Battalion.   I stood at the gate and
watched them march out.   They looked a
most useful lot—fine full-grown men, carrying themselves well—more like a battalion
in India than the regiment of boys one
usually sees at home.

LETTER 2

I ATTENDED yesterday a very historic occasion, and a very touching one. I was one of the group that received the Queen of the Belgians and her family when she landed.

I had no claim to be there, but I get on very well with the harbour master whose dockyard and oil stores I am responsible for, and he took me along. So I found myself in a carriage containing the garrison commander, the Belgian Ambassador, the harbour master, the representative of the Railway, the chief ordnance officer (who had no more claim than I had) and me, being shunted down the pier to receive the Queen.

The ship, a Dutch boat, was timed to meet the submarine picket line at 4. It was close up to time, and, not very long after, she steamed in, her escort waiting outside.

There was no Royal Standard on her. She drew up alongside the pier ; the Ambassador went aboard, saluted by the white- or brown-gloved ship's officers : and then the Queen came along. She looked very sweet, very capable and very charming. Dressed in black, with a white blanket coat, her hair very fair, her eyes very blue (with big rings round them, poor thing !), with very simple, pleasant manners : it brought a lump to the throat when one thought of what all this meant. Three nice, wholesome-looking children were with her, very interested at the journey —two boys of about 10 and 12 and a girl. The boys were fair-haired and blue-eyed like their mother.

They passed to their carriage. Baggage began to be brought along; fat maids struggled with jewel cases and were shepherded in ; and at last they went off, the Queen giving a final smile as we saluted. I shan't forget it in a hurry.

Another boat came to-day, and I went with the harbour master aboard. They had left Antwerp that morning, with a great Zeppelin hovering over the city, bomb-laden. They said she was very high up, that she turned off her engines and floated noiselessly over the forts (at first dawn), then turned them on and steered her course. They said everything fired at her, and that people were warned to keep indoors, as the projectiles fell about. Antwerp is completely dark every night, so as to see the airship better. They said that on that first night she came quite low, above the lighted streets, and aimed at the Bourse, Palace, Barracks, etc., but, not allowing enough for pace, they all dropped ahead. Oh, how they loathed the Germans!

The Queen goes back to-morrow, and they are rather anxious, as some loose floating mines are reported in the Channel. Possibly they are only buoys. I think they will send a boat in front of the Queen's ship, though.

I hear that these last mines in the North Sea were probably laid by a vessel disguised as a French tramp. Pretty low down that.

A few days ago we sent off a second draft (I think my chance of going out is remote at present). I went down to the station to see them off. They were a very fine lot of men, mostly over 30, and sober as judges. Among them were many old friends of mine ; and, while we waited under the gas lamps for the train to go, they talked of old times. "Remember that grey horse of yours on column in Africa, sir ? " " Them manœuvres at Pindi —when we had a night march and then dug till morning—that *was* a night. You dropped your sword, and I had to run after you with it—a good way, too." " That *was* you with the burglar, sir ? I showed it to the guvnor and told him you was my company orficer in India," and so on—little things, all of them, but they gave one a most delightful feeling of friendship. Then a lot of hand-shaking ("Wish I was going with you." " Wish you were coming, sir ") and off they went. I have always known it, but never realized it more than then, that the bond wrought by soldiering is one of the strongest in the world.

We have been working hard at a ring of forts on the hills round. It is rather nice up there early on a clear morning. The Channel has a good many more ships on it than in the first weeks. It was a bare floor of water then ; but, as one hears of German Cavalry pushing down to the coast on the other side, one realizes what it means to us. The importance of being an island suddenly becomes an actuality ; and we seem connected up with the other centuries—the Napoleonic era, the Armada—when the Channel shaped our destinies.

LETTER 3

IT is a long time since I have written. Indeed, I have been very fully occupied. So just a retrospective line or two now.

The most striking thing, of course, here as elsewhere, has been the crowds of recruits, without uniforms, without arms, drilling like mad. They are of all sorts, from cab-runners (only a few) to curates and B.A.'s. Men in well-cut Norfolk jackets, men in broken boots—they become much less interesting as they get into uniform. The curate is a corporal; they say he doesn't hold up his hands at bad language—he just sits on it. One company had a section of University men. The recruits get on quickly on the whole. The battalion is 2000 strong.

On Sunday fortnight we saw the Naval Brigade go off (mostly quite untrained, with

a few weeks' service and nice new kit).
Yesterday they came back. The few I saw
looked as though they had learnt a lot. The
Antwerp trenches under shell fire would
teach them more about soldiering than
much camp exercise.

One of the most impressive things I have
seen since I came here was when the torpedo-
boat flotilla, under the Admiral in a cruiser,
steamed out for action. There wasn't an
action (it was a false alarm), but we thought,
and they thought, there was going to be.
The cruiser got off first, flying strings of
signal flags, and two great Jacks (they don't
fight under the white ensign—it's too like
the German flag). The submarines forged
their way out, the torpedo-boat destroyers
slipped from their moorings one by one,
curveted in the harbour to get opposite
the entrance, and shot off with clouds of
black smoke behind and a great wave in
front. The string of them lengthened out,
the cruiser leading in the distance; and
I don't envy anyone who could have watched
it without a lump in the throat.

There are more searchlights than ever

now, sweeping sky as well as sea ; and they have mounted two aircraft guns. Two German submarines seem to live in the Channel about here. I don't know if the minefield will make a difference. They have had several shots at different ships.

On Sunday I lunched with the General at the Bishop's Palace, where he and his staff live. It is a delightful spot—under the shadow of that wonderful tower. The old part of the palace is attractive, the new cleverly put on. There were no clergy there, but a dozen officers were at lunch, waited on by a butler who looked like St. Anselm, and two very decorous footmen. After lunch, the General and I sat on the lawn between the palace and the Cathedral, and smoked our cigars and talked. It was a glorious afternoon, mellow October, with blue softness over the shadows in the tower, and some flowers still in the borders. The General was in very good form : and he got more and more worked up over various misdemeanours of the War Office and the way he had met them. His language is by no means extreme, but his vocabulary is—military, not episcopal, and I glanced anxiously over my shoulder to see if St. Anselm was gazing in pained reproof out of one of the windows. As far as I could see, however, the Sunday peace remained unbroken. Let us hope St. Anselm slept.

.   .   .   .   .

Orders just received to go to France " forthwith " with four other Captains. So I must put my house in order. I thought it would bring better luck if I got nothing ready beforehand, so I shall have a busy four hours before starting at midday.

I will write as soon as possible from the other side.

LETTER 4

A Port,
October 18*th*, 1914.

I AM still in England. I got as far as Southampton, and was there recalled by wire.
I never felt more utterly depressed and dis-
heartened by anything. It was like physical
pain, and one seemed to be turning back
from the very sound of the guns. I shan't
write any more till I get across. They can't
keep me here much longer.

LETTER 5

LE HAVRE,
Monday, 21st Dec., 1914.

As you know, I started from Waterloo, and got down to Southampton without incident. There I took cab for the Embarkation Office, and went in with some trepidation, after my experience last time. However, all was well—there was no telegram to drag me back, and I was to go on board that evening. They told us the ship did not sail till daylight, that she had sometimes met German submarines, but, being a 20-knotter, was not afraid of them—and that, if the Captain saw one close, he should charge it.

On Sunday morning we woke to find ourselves going down Southampton Water through a lovely dawn, the woods and frosty fields and occasional big houses slipping by. When we got as far as the end of the Isle of Wight, we passed a French destroyer. Her men gave us an English cheer as we went out.

It was a beautiful crossing, rather more roll from the S.W. in the middle of the Channel than I could have wished, but a sunny, delightful day. The white cliffs of France rose, and we steamed along to the brown cliff by Havre.

Some blue-coated red-trousered French soldiers on the end of the breakwater made one realize one was in France at last. Havre looked very pleasant, with its big neat houses and buildings, and villas climbing the hill-side.

We got on shore (having been dealt out four days' rations of biscuits, beef, jam and groceries), and went to report ourselves. I was told to go on to the base camp, but was advised not to take my kit, as it was a sea of mud up there. The advice was excellent : not having my kit with me, I had to return to sleep at this hotel.

It was Belgian day here yesterday : and really very nicely turned out young women kept on asking one to buy flags (little paper ones on pins). I didn't mean to get more than one : but was ultimately reduced to 1d. for my tram fare back.

All I learnt at the camp was that there was a good draft of the Regiment there, which I should probably take up. My hopes were (alas, wrongly) roused. I trammed back, had a drink on the pavement at a café, and watched the crowds. These were large, being Sunday, and included a lot of soldiers with their relations —apple-cheeked old peasant women in white winged caps ; also wives and children—and the ordinary prosperous civilian and family.

I came back and dined with a friend, and so to bed.

This morning I took my kit to the foot of the hill where the camp is, climbed up, leaving it in a shop, past the exquisite little Norman church half-way up, and waded through the sea of mud of which the camp (canvas) consists, only to hear that I was posted to a strange Regiment, and must leave this afternoon.

Of course this is an awful blow. I know nothing of them, officers, men, or manners. They know nothing of me—I shall be the

c

new boy, with all my way to make with everybody. However, there it is—I can't help it.

I report myself at Rouen this evening, and then the world is all before me.

I think one feels one is on the verge of a very great test. I hope this day week I shall have done decently.

LETTER 6

A Farmhouse behind the Trenches,
France,
*Boxing Day Night—*7 *p.m.*

Here I am at last. " Boom ! " went a distant biggish gun then. " Plick—plock " went an occasional rifle when I looked out just now. The trenches are a mile or so away and we go up there to-morrow.

I am writing in the large room of a goodish farmhouse. Our servants, the family, and a rather surly subaltern of two months' service, who prefers it, are in the kitchen next door. The house and outbuildings are round the farmyard, in a quadrangle ; and there the whole of my company, or at least the 170 here, are billeted. The men are snugly stowed in the barns and lofts.

There is a crucifix in nearly every room and Madonnas between the family photos on the wall. The house has one corner

19

bitten off by a shell. I have spent the last hour in proving (successfully) that the fire can be lit (the S.S. in the kitchen only produced a room full of coal smoke when I told him to try) and now sit down beside the said fire to write to you.

I went up to Rouen on Monday, and there had a pleasant surprise.

You know my silver cigar case the burglar bagged ? It was won for me by my pony in India. Well, when I left him in the stable at Peshawar, certainly the last place I expected to meet him next would have been a Normandy farm, but there he was. Close to the Infantry base camp was the Indian depot ; old John, whom you know, of the 1st Battalion, was Adjutant of it, and he had brought the pony with him.

It was delightful meeting John—one of the old lot in a strange land and me on my way to complete strangers. He lunched with me, and then I went over to his camp.

This was extremely well run, and a little bit of India. Every sort of man was there —Sikh and Gurkha, Pathan and Punjabi

Mussulman. They were just having a parade
to see who smoked, for the Princess's gift.
A smart little Gurkha Adjutant was running
them. I shook him warmly by the hand
when John introduced me (as was expected),
and aired my exiguous Hindustani. All the
Gurkhas smoked of course, and most of the
others. Then came a football match —
Gurkhas v. Pathans (John insists on a
match every day), the native Adjutant
doing umpire. He wasn't the least fair :
but no one expected him to be. They played
with great zeal. " Maro ! maro ! charge
kuro ! " (Hit ! hit ! make a charge !) they
kept shouting. Meanwhile a small Gurkha
with a very large grin came up to us as I
was showing off my torch. " Each German
had one," he said. We asked about it.
" Oh," he said, " we took 104 and killed
40 more. I came to a Major " (he pointed
to the crown on the Commandant's shoulder)
" and he tried to draw his revolver : but I
was too quick." " With your kukri ? "
asked the Commandant. " Yes," he said,
" and then he dropped his revolver and
asked for mercy. I brought him in." And

he smiled all over. The Pathans were just then making a great noise over the game. " Listen to these country-people! " he said confidentially, though what he called himself I don't know. Just then a company of blue-coated, red-trousered French troops went swinging down the road, singing—a pleasant sort of folk-tune, better class than the stuff our men sing, and in softer, more educated voices, though without the same roaring go. It made a curious picture altogether—the poplar-bordered road, the Frenchmen, the turbaned and unturbaned Indians, the familiar Indian followers, the six little kitchens for the six castes, each railed off, with men kneading things in sponge baths—John's substitute for native cooking paraphernalia.

Next day I was on fatigue at the docks, taking a couple of hundred men down to unload stores. These were largely oats— a present from Alberta, each sack labelled " Alberta's gift." I lunched at a pastry-cook's opposite the Cathedral, going to look at it first. The front is wonderful—delicate lace work in stone. The iron spire, very tall and slender, is very successful, all but a sort of summer-house thing at the top. There was an altar inside draped with the French, British and Belgian flags.

Next morning I was warned to go at mid-day. We marched down to the station on a perfect day, and waited there three hours. A clear sky, a tendency to frost, an afternoon wintry sun, bright on Rouen spires— it was very inspiriting. At the station the King and Queen's Christmas card was dealt out to us. Its direct simplicity went straight home. I know it is very much appreciated, for I have been censoring the men's letters this morning. There is a personal note about it that I find very touching.

It was Christmas Eve—and we were on our way, about a dozen officers of different corps and 1300 men, though no men for here. We were four in one carriage; the light went out, and I produced a candle and a petrol lamp I got at Rouen. Over the latter we brewed some toddy.

I woke at dawn of Christmas Day—an ideal Christmas morning. We were nearing Calais; the fields were white with frost, the dykes ice-covered, the sky clear, the East red. As we neared Calais the boom of the great Cathedral bell rang over the place.

I had some cocoa, and we made a brew with hot water from an engine. On—and I went on reading the Christmas Carol, which I had started the evening before. We got nearer the Front. Occasional trenches appeared in the fields. A party of girls were hurrying to church : and on the same road great howitzers were coming along behind traction engines. At last we reached railhead and got out.

It was a small town, seven miles behind the lines. There was not much sign of war. Motor cars with staff officers came along. We detrained, and the men made tea in the field before starting to march the seven or eight miles to our destination.

We could hear the boom of distant guns. Cheery people came to afternoon service past us as we had our meal. Then we marched out.

A house or two shattered by shell fire was all that showed it was not peace. Evening fell, and we fetched up at another little town, the base of this section. Here the men went off to their units, and we were to billet for the night. " We " were five officers for this battalion.

We were pretty weary, having carried our packs and equipment like the men (only no rifle), and at first our billets were delusive. We marched an extra mile or so, and the prospect of Christmas Dinner seemed remote indeed. By some mistake we were wandering into open fields in a wrong direction. But at last we fetched up at a house in the town belonging to a most kindly Frenchwoman. She and a friend set about cooking us dinner—pork chops and potatoes. We spread our valises upstairs. I produced all my candles for illumination. After dinner we brewed some rum punch out of ration rum, in which we drank " absent friends."

We turned in, dog tired. Before that I heard " God save the King " being sung at the close of some Tommies' concert. It has wonderful meanings, sometimes.

The owner of the house told us that her husband was fighting somewhere, and that she had left the town when the Germans came, and returned to find all her bedding and her husband's clothes gone, her coal burnt, and a wounded German in the front room among piles of cinders. At least she did not find him, because the English removed him just before.

We walked out here on Boxing Day morning—four miles through most beautiful crisp sunny hard winter weather. I was put to a company of 220 men, which I command for the moment in this attractive farmhouse. They were very kind and friendly, and I feel I am in for a most interesting job, in spite of being away from the Regiment. This battalion is practically being made anew out of officers from everywhere and reserves from England, and I am responsible for making one quarter of it.

27th December.

I must finish this letter off, as it is already so huge. Next time I will tell you of the night alarm last night and of the pleasant old farm lady here.

On Christmas Day there was an armistice

along here.   There was an English funeral
service in the space between the lines which
a lot of German officers and men reverently
attended.   I am told there was a football
match in another place.

LETTER 7

I⊤ is called the Aquarium because of the
pretty arrangement of drip fountains and
pools. It is a dug-out—and dug, as all these
trenches are, in clay soil. The Germans
know it, and snipe it (harmlessly); but they
think it is only a store, and don't shell it.
They want to be on good terms with us.
Last night I hear they shouted across that
they were fed up and hoped it would stop
soon, and would anyone play them at football.

I never conceived dirt like this. These
are narrow clay ditches, 5 to 6 feet deep,
2 feet 6 inches to 3 feet wide. It has
rained ever since we arrived last night. I
feel like an eel in the aquarium, and am
covered with the same sort of slime. (I
move to avoid a drip.)

They snipe certain points; and I am going up to the forward sap after lunch to see if I can pick off anything.

Perhaps a bald diary will show you the sort of thing.

2 p.m. yesterday. Came out before the troops, with the C.O., to see the trenches we were to take over. Four hours' solid plodding in every warm garment I possess, along slimy clay passages that your elbows rub, and through clay mud from 3 inches deep, up to impassable. I sweated like a pig, carrying my pack. Suggested that the men should be called " His Majesty's Mudlarks." Jest rather a success.

6 p.m. Back to my post here. Troops beginning to come in. Men literally foundered and blocked the road; I spent a strenuous two hours on the surface (safe now, though just sniped occasionally) throwing in planks and tins for the men to tread on, and helping out foundered men. One man I had to leave; I don't know if he's out yet.

8–11 p.m. Looking round my lot. The surly (and only) subaltern, much improved,

is on a detached post, so I have to do it
all. Awful walking. Had some jam sand-
wiches I brought up with me. Rations not
in yet.

12 m.n. Out reconnoitring from my
forward sap. The Germans are, say, 300
yards from there ; I went, say, 150. People
go much closer ; but I don't know the
country yet. Took two volunteers with me.
Misty moonlight, all clear, rain followed.

1 a.m. Ploughed back a quarter of a mile
to a post under me (shoved on to me since
dark). Howling hurricane. Seas of mud.

2 a.m. Called the Sergeant-Major ; turned
in till 5 a.m. Then out. Pitch black. The
men have to " stand to arms." Had to go
round with torch, poking them out. Bitter
and driving rain. Got them all on to parapet.
Sent out listening post. Waited for dawn,
6.30. All clear. Trenches water-logged.

9 a.m. The General and gilded staff came
round, after a night in bed and a comfortable
breakfast. Picked a lot of small holes. I
was amused.

LETTER 8

The Aquarium,
The Trenches,
3 *a.m., New Year's Day.*

A HAPPY New Year to every one! The
Germans, a few hundred yards away, have
been wishing us all seasonable wishes by
turning on a friendly and harmless fire of
maxims and rifles across the intervening
field, to which demonstration, accompanied
as it was with choruses, cheering, and a
cornet playing the Austrian Hymn and bits
of other things, we did not even pay the
compliment of standing to arms; except
that a Scotch Regiment, which also keeps
New Year's day, cheered and fired with
great enthusiasm. It was a curious effect,
looking over the parapet : our lines, silent
and dark, the men standing about very
much amused; the German lines one big
roar of jovial sound, with fires blazing in

31

places behind them, and the constant crackle of bullets going overhead. This was soon after 11 o'clock ; but their time is an hour ahead. Now all is absolutely still. A single shot came over then ; beyond the parapet it is all grey mystery.

I think every one would have felt it wasn't playing the game to attack them to-night.

That is one of the odd features of this. There is really a great bond of sympathy between the two sides, because no one can understand the sufferings of the one like the other. In the armistice the other day I believe the Germans made no bones at all about being extremely fed up with the life, though they still think they will win. They regarded us as the real enemy they are fighting, and when asked why they were so bitter against us, said, " Well, what can you expect ? We should have managed the other two, but for you."

This trench existence is rather wearing. The first three days I only got 4 hours' sleep a day, if that. Not having a subaltern here, I divide the night with the Sergeant-Major (to-night he took the first half), but

then something turns up in the other half
that one has to do ; and the day is pretty
full somehow—inspecting rifles which get
constantly caked with mud, trying to keep
the pathways passable, eluding the sniper,
and visiting the post behind. (They are
extraordinarily keen on sniping, thou;h it
seems a silly game, doing them no good
really and us no harm.) Then one always
has to stand to at 5.30 a.m.

In the daytime this is a life of one dimen-
sion : you cannot go upwards or sideways,
only along. Even in dry weather one gets
tired of the endless vista of narrow walls,
firing recesses and sleeping holes on one
side, little fireplaces and such on the other.
In wet weather it is dreadful—sticky boggy
clay to walk through, slimy walls to rub
against. You get coated in clay from head
to foot.

And these are luxurious trenches. What
life must have been like in trenches dug
hurriedly on the field of battle and held
against constant attacks I can hardly
imagine.

When darkness falls we resume our three

D

dimensions. Rations come in over the back ;
men go to get water more freely. The advanced post relief walks boldly out, instead
of having to creep along a sap half full of
water. Even then you have to be careful,
though. I told a sentry to get over the
parapet and go to the wire for something
the other evening. Immediately there was
" crack-crack," and a couple of bullets
whizzed by, soon followed by some more.
I tried holding up a coat and hat on a rifle,
and they fired at that. Thinking it might be
a sniper in our territory, I took out a few
men to try and snaffle him. We started
from a flank and crept along a ditch. Several
willow logs seemed as if they were going to
be Germans, but weren't —he wasn't in the
trees we had suspected. I crawled on my
front over the sticky field to see if there was
a German post among some manure heaps,
deposited some time ago and never spread.
But there wasn't, and we went back,
having at least shown our ground was clear.
The firers were probably a covering party
for their R.E., whom we could hear working
a little way off.

In front of the lines we have what are called T-headed saps—curly cuttings to walk along under cover, ending in a small trench for an observation post.   These must almost overlap the German ones sometimes.   I have one about 150 yards in front of our trench.   This is a retired bit, so the head of the sap is still 200 yards or so from the Germans.

The other night the Regiment next this one took it into its head the Germans were going to attack, and stood to arms.   While we were discussing this, a man came in from my forward sap, and said, " Fifty Germans creeping towards us through the cabbages " (i.e. beet).   I didn't much believe in this ; but it seemed to chip in with the other Regiment's idea, so I went out along the sap to see what they had to say.   I found it was all nonsense—four or five men of one of our patrols had been along.   I spoke, I suppose, rather loud and clear to the men on the post, because, suddenly, from the direction of the German trenches came a cry of " *Machingewehr !* "   I don't know if they thought *I* was an attack coming off.

I walked back with a slightly ticklish feeling in the small of the back, hoping they would not open fire at the sound of the voice.

We leave the trenches to-morrow, and go into reserve for a bit. There we get a chance of cleaning up, and also doing a bit of training. After the Ypres fighting this Regiment consisted of four officers and seventy-five men.

It is quite still now, and it will be till dawn. Before that we shall " stand to " — every man at his place on the parapet, peering over, his rifle and bayonet alongside. Then the light will grow, the few fields and willow-edged ditches we are concerned with will take shape : " Plick-plock " will go the first sniper. Then a few more will chip in ; then it will be full day, all but the sentries will stand down, the men will gather over their little fires, and the daily round will be started.

By the way, I was going to tell you about the people at our last billet. It was a substantial farm. The old farmer's wife was a dear old thing —very active, and very friendly. She insisted on doing one's washing free. I sat in the kitchen one wet morning, and she fussed around and talked, and spoke of her son, " malheureusement blessé " (with a little choke, poor old thing). The Army Doctor came in—a great friend of hers—and they discussed his various local patients; he seems to attend half the country-side, as well as the men. "And how is the little Suzanne ? and Marie ? " and so on. Then she produced for us bowls of warm milk, and the Doctor went to sleep, having been up on the night show the evening before. Nothing happened on the latter, by the way ; we expected an attack, but something went wrong. Both sides blazed at each other, the guns made a great noise, Roman candle stars fired out of sort of pistols lit up the scene, but that was all. We were in reserve, packed the men in a barn near the firing line, unpacked them in the morning and marched home. My subalterns were very late turning out when we got the alarm, and I found they had had the cheek to sleep in pyjamas—a practice I told them must cease.

It's five o'clock ; I must go and squelch up the trench and have a look at things, and in half an hour they must " stand to." Nothing will happen, though.

LETTER 9

We left the trenches on New Year's Day, at dusk. It was a wet and beastly evening —a good time to leave. The various platoons climbed out at the back and made their own way over squudgy fields, subject to the attentions of the harmless necessary sniper. By the way, one notices one great difference between this and South Africa. One never hears the whine of a comparatively long-range bullet going past, it is always the sharp crack of close range—such as I heard when my horse was killed. When it passes at all close it is like a revolver let off by your ear. The instinctive duck is amusing, because, of course, if you hear it the thing is past.

I collected the company behind some straw stacks (or rather stacks of unthreshed and rotting wheat) in a ruined farm behind the lines. In the orchard are some British graves, with crucifixes from the walls of the house at their heads, and rudely written inscriptions at their feet.

My platoon sergeants are not very expert, and managed to lose some men on the way : however, eventually we collected, and joined the battalion. Then we marched to billets (not these).

It was very delightful being on the surface again, and free, and very comforting to reach a room with a firm floor and a fire — particularly when it came on to rain hard. One went to sleep thinking snugly of the trenches.

Billets are all much the same — the square courtyard round the manure heap, the barns, the deep eaves under which men can fall in when it is wet, the kitchen where the family and farm-hands ive, and our meals are cooked, the living room and one or two bedrooms for the officers, with many crucifixes and pictures of the Virgin. We made a combined Mess of the officers of two companies, and did very well.

The next day or two were peaceful and

rainy. The men cleaned themselves up a trifle (we were all simply plastered with mud) and got their rifles clean. We did a route march or two, past pretty old 17th century moated farmhouses, over incredibly heavy land. A vigorous cannonade one night (by our guns) brought me from my bed, expecting to be turned out, but we weren't. To-day we moved back here, preparatory to returning to the trenches (which must be nearly flooded), and on the way the battalion had a bath.

This bath is an extraordinarily good scheme. In the little town just behind us is a large laundry—not working, of course. Here the troops have hot baths, fifty at a time : this battalion was easily done to-day. There are endless supplies of hot water from the laundry arrangements. The wash tubs make bath tubs. Barbers are up above, cropping the men. My men, by the way, insisted on having that horrible forelock left on, so I just stood them up in a row, each platoon before it left, and went with the barber down the line, lopping it off as they stood.

I had a glorious bath myself. The officers' part contains a long tin bath for soaking and washing, and two great vats, hot and cold, for plunging. The hot vat is five feet deep and six feet across—simply glorious. The cold one was *very* cold, but bucked one up. After paddling round and round in the hot one for ten minutes, a short sharp shock just set one up.

I trekked back here in the dark and rain, and found the company installed, and most of them out on fatigue, digging. This can only be done at night, near the trenches. Half are now in (10.30 p.m.)—the rest will return at midnight probably. I don't expect we shall be disturbed to-night. I hope not.

The old lady here welcomed us back very cordially. We are old friends now.

LETTER 10

It amuses me now to think of my complaints about the Aquarium. I thought when I last wrote that I knew something about mud and trench discomfort. I hadn't even touched the fringe of the subject.

We are back in the trenches, and I am in another part. It is so flooded as only to be occupiable in patches, completely isolated by day, as all the communication trenches are rivers. (By the way, our works have dammed a brook that flows from the German trenches, and backed it up into them.) One comes out at dusk, and arrives in the dark in a sea of very heavy clay mud, scarred by a maze of deep cuts filled with water—formerly trenches. Some of these you jump, without confidence, others you go round. Officers appear out of the darkness and say

43

they have so many men here or there to be relieved. You scatter out your 150 men, and soon find yourself, completely confused, with a few men under your hand, and the rest goodness knows where. Last night was one long nightmare of dragging foot after foot out of the heavy gluey soil, finding ever new uninviting-looking chasms, and making frantic and incorrect calculations as to where one was. In addition to other joys, the men had to be kept at work on fresh trenches to replace these flooded ones, all night. Also rations and water for the day had to be laid in.

With full light, all above-ground activity ceases. We stood to arms for an hour before dawn and presently a beautiful day began.

The state of dirt one was in was simply indescribable. Everything is wet sticky clay, or, where it has been churned enough, a rich clay-cream. In the dark one stumbles and staggers and falls down, till really one is literally coated from head to foot. I haven't felt the real skin of my hands to-day.

The state of this particular bit of partially flooded trench is pretty bad. In parts you

sink over your knees : outside the kennel
(4 ft. × 4 ft. dug-out, lined appropriately
with straw) a tide of liquid clay 3 inches
deep rolls.

The sun rises, and the early sniper begins.
The German lines are 300 yards away, and
we search for movement at which to reply.
Between us is a no man's land —crops sown
that will never be gathered, other crops still
more lately sown and marked with crosses,
ditches, trees, dead sheep. Behind both
lines, ruined farmhouses, their roofs mere
skeletons of rafters.

And all, to-day, under a delicious sun,
soft and spring-like.

I tried a hand at sniping. I did not see
anyone, so fired at the basins full of water
being hurled out of their trenches by baling
Germans. At the same time I felt sympa-
thetic. I watched one man through glasses
this morning, but was not in time with the
rifle.

I slept a bit in the afternoon, and about
sunset finished up the day by testing the
" Verey's Pistol " here—a pistol that fires a
brilliant Roman candle ball at the opposite

trenches. The Germans took it as it was
meant, and " Ah'd " it like a firework, as it
sailed over.

With dark the muddy chase began again,
looking up the scattered platoons and ar-
ranging various matters. It rapidly became
pitch dark and rained. One felt more hope-
less and homeless than ever.

All that is the lighter side—my best
sergeant and a rather truculent private were
shot dead during the day. We buried them
after dark.

LETTER 11

I GOT quite to like the Kennel. I got some
clean straw for it, and learnt how to curl up
in it; with a mackintosh sheet over the
opening it was quite snug. I got a bit of
the trench into rather better condition —
cleared out the mud, and baled constantly.
We had several fine days, though the nights
were bad. But the mud outside remained a
nightmare. At dusk we began to wake up:
ration parties went out, the sick went up to
the Doctor, various jobs on the parapet were
taken in hand, and I stumbled and floundered
through the clinging mud, up and down wet
clay banks, over yawning chasms (really
quite narrow, but horrid in the dark), and
found my isolated posts. (The only advantage of the floods was that the General
could not get at one in the day.) And all the

time there was the crack overhead of the bullet of the inevitable sniper : they have fixed rifles for night work.

This sniping is really very odd. I think we regard it as merely foolish, and bad form. It serves no military end whatever ; one or two poor devils get knocked out by day : by night they hardly ever hit anyone. If their idea is to create alarm or nervousness they fail completely, for, as I said, no one takes any notice of it. The men laugh at it during the daytime. They become careful how they move, but that is all. The Germans must have a most carefully organized system, with permanent snipers with telescopic sights ; they fire an immense lot of ammunition, and effect nothing of the slightest value. We had a tame sniper opposite my dug-out. You could always draw him by firing at his home —rather like the old story of " And that " (throwing a stone at his window) " is the Master."

I think we feel rather contemptuous of the elaborate pains taken over something so futile. On the whole, it is rather good practice for the raw hands, being under fire.

The Germans demonstrate much more than we do, altogether. They fire a lot of the Roman candle stars I spoke of, that come lobbing over to our trenches. They do this while our troops are moving, but never spot anyone. The other night a man bringing down a biscuit tin got a bullet through it, and at the same time one of these lights came floating across. This was too much for him. Calling out " I'm not going to be turned into a ruddy little twinkling star for them," he hurled the box away, and dropped into the trench.

They are funny devils. A corporal, taking up the ration party the other night, held a review of his seven men before he had gone far. " Men," said the corporal, " you are the finest body of troops I have ever had the pleasure of reviewing," and more to the same effect. Perhaps it calmed them ! He is now known as the " General."

They even open with Maxims on the sound of the relieving parties (for nothing will induce our men to do anything quietly). One of my subalterns was so treated coming out this time. He was new —a very good chap

E.

though. " The men went plodding on," he said, " so I did the same. They fired 100 rounds, but it all went pretty high." Of course all this is very good for them.

We hope that the black silence with which we treat all this gets on their nerves—no stars, no Maxims, no shooting.

The other night I patrolled between the lines with a corporal—a very good man. The nights are quite dark—just faint starlight that evening, with a touch of frost. We went cautiously out, lying down and looking along the ground at intervals. I must say at first it is very creepy. Once outside the wire, the German lines are perhaps 350 yards off, their advanced saps much less. We had orders not to fire that night, as our working parties were digging behind the trenches, and they did not want to draw fire on them. As soon as we got out we could hear the splash of the Germans baling. We crept forward, and across a little brook, then knelt and looked round the sky-line. We could hear their Engineers working on their wire, and we could hear every word the men in the trench in front were saying : very

cheery they seemed too. It is the only
time I have wished I knew German. The
field had just a " bone " in it —just a little
stiffening with the frost ; and we peered
through the grey blank. Then one of the
Germans struck up on a mouth organ —
rather well —and another sang a bar or two.
Then I thought I spotted a German patrol
of six men coming our way (I have reason to
think now it was a row of willow trees and
nerves), and retired hastily a little way. Then
after a sideways movement along our own
wire, where we were seen by, and had some
difficulty in satisfying a sentry (we dropped
down and said who we were, and he refused
to say whether he was satisfied or not !) we
went home.

I thought I had been sitting almost on the
German position ; but next morning I saw
I wasn't half-way across, or perhaps just.

I'm not proud of the performance, but
there it is, bald and unvarnished.

I'm inclined to think all round, that we
are worst at the Unknown and best at the
Known : that we are more imaginative than
is usually allowed, and that our forte is

taking on considerable odds once they have
developed.

.   .   .   .   .

I must say the supplies of everything are
very good. They are giving the men a
certain number of gum boots in the trenches,
and leather knee boots for the officers.

I had rather an amusing experience one
night. As you know, our feet are sopping
for four days on end, and pretty cold. Before
we went in last time the Doctor warned me
to be careful of a rubbed heel, which he said
was the place for trouble to begin —frost-bite
to wit. " This is where it would be taken
off," he said, drawing a line round my ankle
with his finger. The second night I found
my foot swollen and painful, and sent up a
note to him, really for advice. My servant,
with the sensationalism of his race, gave the
Doctor such an account of it that he promptly
despatched four stretcher bearers with orders
to bring me up ! At midnight I started off,
hanging on to the necks of two of them over
the quagmire and getting comfortably into
the stretcher as soon as we got to the road
(after a time the stretcher bearers grunted

a bit). It was a beautiful starlight n:ght, and what struck me most was the new view of the sky one got lying on one's back. I never saw so much of it before. We trekked on down the road for three-quarters of a mile and arrived at the dressing station—a little farm. We woke the Doctor, who came and had a look. " Just drawn by the wet," he said, " I'll give them a rub with vaseline." He offered me 24 hours out, but I wanted to get back. He got a fire going, and provided tea, eggs, bread and butter. I washed and shaved and had a meal and pushed off just in time to walk back to the trenches before daylight. Altogether a very pleasant night. It was a fine dawn too, with the new moon reflected with the poplar trees in the flooded ditches.

The other evening I was sent out with 100 men to support a working party. (The Germans were working that night too, I believe, and the covering parties in front were watching each other in the dark, 30 yards off. They could see the reliefs every hour, but disregarded each other.) This was *not* a good evening. I started by putting one leg completely into the cesspool of the farmyard of the ruined farm we were at. I couldn't bear myself for hours ; my new trench boot was full. I opened it and stood hopefully in the wind, without much effect. One of my posts complained of being near an old dead cow —I couldn't smell it.

" Fritz " was playing about the road all night. Fritz is the fixed rifle of the Kaiserin Augusta Guard, opposite. He did no damage. I supped at the H.Q. of the section ; it had been a pub, with automatic machines round the wall, silver balls in front of the mirrors, and printed rules as to drink and other things hanging round. The drink provided, by the way, was very good : some one had been sent some home-made sloe gin. We trekked back just before day-light.

We are back in our old billet, and very pleasant it is. I think the first day is the best —the contrast between the fire, the hard floor, the dryness, and the mess and mud you have just left. Also the getting into clothes that are not coated with mud. One's fingers get rather sore with the con-

stant wetting and drying; you can't wash
the clay off—it merely becomes slime. You
dry it and partially scrape it. No towel
could survive attempts to wash, and clean
water in the trenches is very precious.

The trenches were more interesting this
time than last, as we were in closer personal
touch with the Germans. Being new to it,
I started by laying myself out to get a man
(a cook, I think) who fairly often appeared
at a dug-out opposite (I didn't get him). I
now think that is a poor game, and shall
confine myself to snipers. Of course, having
had two men killed made me want to get
some one. I had another man rather badly
hit just before we got out, due to the parapet
falling in with the rain.

LETTER 12

Marie Louise has just gone. She put her
head round the door of the kitchen to say
good-bye to me. She is a cheery soul of 18,
and looked in this afternoon to have a
gossip with our Marie—same age—on her
way to take possession of her own people's
house again. This is in a wrecked village,
considerably nearer the firing line. I told
her to look out for shells—she said she was
not afraid of them. I asked her if the roof
was on and she said yes, but broken. I said
no doubt she had an umbrella, and she
laughed again. They are wonderfully pleasant, simple-mannered, frank people. When
Marie Louise arrived, Marie was doing her
hair at the glass over the settle. Madame
(whom Marie, and consequently our servants,
call "*maman*") was stitching a new sack-
ing apron; two of our servants were washing

up (I must say they behave very nicely with the people of the house), and we were at the lunch table at one end of the room, which we pretend is a different room altogether. I have given up attempting to keep state in the dank and dark room next door, with its broken windows, and its fireplace in which no efforts will make a fire burn. On the stove, then, now, and almost always, stews the cows' dinner.

" Marie," said my servant then, " got any offs ? " His accent is really most disappointing, seeing the practice he has, and was too much for Marie. " Oofs," corrected the scholar among the party. Then Marie understood, and nodded. " Lay, charbon, pang and burr " do not present such difficulties.

By the way, all conversation has been punctuated by rounds fired by the howitzer battery at the next farm. It is when the Germans search for that that this farm is endangered.

The curé was in this morning, and I had a talk with him—also an attractive figure. His is the ruined church. He redecorated it a year or two ago, and had flourishing schools. I said it would resurrect, he said it would take many years. He said he had a XVI century plaque which was melted among the debris on the floor.

There is a fine old church near here, not damaged. I met the vicar the other day. I was looking for one of our people in his churchyard. He was rather like the Bishop in the "Bishop's Move"—a nice old white-haired man. Our Army chaplain—a very good chap—is a great pal of his, and uses his house.

That same chaplain had service last Sunday. I never heard "Noël" sung with such a volume of sound.

Last night I was out all night in support at the same ruined farm. Half the night we were trench digging as well, to a tremendous accompaniment of artillery fire from our guns, a little way off. Flash—flash—flash—pause—bang—bang—bang—constantly. I don't know what they were firing at. I thought they might invite reprisals, but nothing happened.

To-morrow we go back into the trenches —to-night I dig again.

LETTER 13

I SUPPOSE a month or two ago one would
have thought the following uniform odd :

(1) A purple woollen turban with a black
button atop, over

(2) a brown woollen helmet, a delicate
oval left for the face.

(3) A uniform greatcoat, worn *négligé* over

(4) a long-haired Japanese fur coat.

That, however, is the kit of one of the men
outside, and it is a common type. These
woollen things have certainly been an immense comfort to the men. We have had
a very quiet time in the trenches this
time.

I am back at the Aquarium (a foot of
water in it every morning). The Germans
are much further off than in the last place,

and very quiet. We have had no rain,
though the trench is in a shocking state of
mud and water. The parapet keeps falling
in ; 'and the floor has been constantly raised
with earth from the sides, in mistaken efforts
to get it dry. It would be a very uncomfortable trench to be badly sniped in. I made a
new trench at the back of the old one on a
higher level, and got some relief.

We have had some rifle practice at various
objects on the German trenches. They are
quite ready to mark for us, waving a spade
across the target (a machine-gun plate).
Our shooting, observed through our telescope, was quite unexpectedly good, even at
long ranges.

They turned a rather distant Maxim on
to us one night, getting us in enfilade. It did
not do any damage, but I must say it
startled me. I was walking out to a forward
sap at the time, and rapidly went to ground,
arriving at the sap-head almost on all fours.
The bullets were coming from such a very
odd direction —the line makes a great curve
here, and they were firing almost from the
rear.

I have started a company scout section for patrolling purposes, and find it answers very well. One is an old poacher, another was a scout in South Africa—most of them know something about it, and they are keen.

LETTER 14

LAST night the moon was about three-quarters. I came out of the C.O.'s dug-out at Support Farm for the third or fourth time, on my way to the trench in front, in an endeavour to meet his views about holding ' the line. (His dug-out reminds me of harvest festival : it is lined with stooks of unthreshed wheat from the stack near.) Clouds were chasing across, the skeleton trees were silhouetted against the sky and the few remaining walls of the farm made a black patch. I squelched on.

I wasn't feeling very extraordinarily bright, having a temperature of 102°; and it had been rather a worrying evening. We went into the trenches under a new distribution in absolutely inky darkness, before the moon rose—real blackness, where you

could not see your feet. The arrangements
went wrong ; the other Regiment did not
roll up in sufficient strength. Also the C.O.
got anxious about a gap in the line that no
one had minded before. Also new trenches
had to be got under way to replace water-
logged ones, and the men who should have
brought two or three sandbags apiece, un-
accountably, had next to none. Also it
came on an absolute downpour of rain.
Also the subaltern turned quite brainless.
The one redeeming feature was the German
illumination.

Every five minutes they sent up one of '
their brilliant stars, which threw a little
cheeriness over the scene, and in between
they played about with their searchlights.

At last, however, everything got more or
less in train—the moon rose, the C.O.'s
qualms were satisfied, and about midnight
I walked back here to the dressing station as
I had promised the Doctor to do. This morning he says, influenza and very slight con-
gestion of the lung—meaning three weeks
at some base.

In the Train on the way to Boulogne.

It's no good. I can't connect up the two worlds at all : this one of light and comfort and cleanliness and orderlies coming to press little meals on you and a Sister with eau-de-Cologne for your handkerchief, and that other one (two nights' distant by mere time) of mud and snipers.

When I got back to the dressing station (about three-quarters of a mile back) the Doctor had one of the farmhouse beds ready for me. I mistrust these on principle ; however, he guaranteed it, and was very proud of having supplied it with sheets. It was a stuffy feather bed filling up most of a tiny room. Some one had bunged up the broken window, and I unbunged it, and slept most of the following morning, being still 102°. I trekked on in the afternoon (in a cart) to the next rung of the hospital ladder —the bearer division in the village behind. Thence I was passed on in a motor to the next village, where I spent a delicious night in the best bedroom of a nice house (headquarters of the next rung —the Tent Division) nicely furnished, and with flickering fire-light on the walls and ceiling. Thence by motor this morning to railhead, where I spent a pleasant day in a sunny ward. Here I was marked up as a stretcher case (a technical distinction, I think, but I jibbed at coming into the train through the window) and sent off to-night.

Influenza apart, I believe I am already better for the change, short time as I have done. The old world had got too far out of the perspective. I will close this now and write again from the base.

BOULOGNE, *February 5th*, 1915.

P.S.—I hear I cross to-morrow, so will bring this letter with me and post it at home. It is a real joy here—a sunny fresh day, a pleasant room with a pleasant mate, a good bath, books, and every one most kind. Indeed, I have been very much touched by the kindness, tenderness really, every one has shown all through.

F

LETTER 15

A Port,
April, 1915.

I DO not find anything very much changed here. The Kitchener battalions are obviously finding themselves. The spy mania seems to have died down. I saw a Zepp the other night. It did no harm; but it made me feel very angry. That silvery malignant thing over England seemed a sort of defilement.

One hears accounts of the Neuve Chapelle fight. It seems that the mist came down and stopped our cavalry getting through.

Our lot were in it again at Aubers Ridge, and more of the men I know well have been killed. It is awful how the list grows. But staying at home gets badly on one's nerves.

LETTER 16

B.E.F.,

6th June, 1915.

HERE I am, in clover, for the moment. The
Headquarters of the Brigade are in this
town, in a beautiful house standing in a
small walled garden. The rhododendrons
are out, and roses : this hot day the flowers
and little lawns looked deliciously cool. We
live in a big stone hall, with a fine oak
staircase, and nice pictures and tapestry on
the walls. There are other pleasant rooms
too. A greater contrast to the dirty farmhouse from which I started home in February
could not be imagined. Outside there is a
pretty provincial town, with red-roofed
houses and a market square, from the middle
of which rises an old stone clock tower, with
a great gold dragon as vane. The ordinary
French population goes its ordinary ways,
and but for three things it might be peace

time : the street corners and the *estaminets* are full of khaki, a great observation balloon glistens yellow in the sun, and the guns are rumbling all the time.

This is going to be a very interesting job, though of course I haven't really started it yet. I have all the machine-guns of the five Regiments of the Brigade to look after. The General and his staff are extremely pleasant. My kit, however, is not up to staff standard, being based on the necessities of the trenches. I feel rather like a chap who, having dressed for salmon fishing, finds himself at a dance.

We crossed yesterday in a cold thick fog that delayed the boat some hours. I had an excellent dinner at Boulogne, and took my place in the train soon afterwards. It didn't start till four, but I got in a good sleep. I roused before we got to St. Omer. It was a wonderful contrast to my arrival up country last year. Then a cold red sun was rising over frosty fields, while the big bell of Calais boomed for the Christmas Mass. This time the hayfields and cornfields lay deep in the warm sunshine. Being Sunday, the bell of the village church was ringing at each place where we stopped.

It was curious, crossing in the fog, the way we picked up other vessels. Sirens would answer, first faint, then louder, and our engines be stopped. Then, like a sigh of relief, came from the bridge —" There she is ! " and a boat would shape itself out of the fog. We had plenty of room, but I fancy the Captain did not hit the coast of France just where he expected.

One noticed enormous trains of motor lorries on the way up. There were at least 100 in the first I saw.

Altogether this is very good indeed. I feel able to enjoy the fine day in a way I did not feel at liberty to at home !

They say the Germans have their tails down in this part of the world.

LETTER 17

Waterloo Day, 1915,
NORTHERN FRANCE.

I WILL write you as full an account as I can
of our fight on June 15–16 (Quatre Bras
centenary).

And first, I am left with a feeling of awe
and reverence for the way in which British
officers and men (quite ordinary, all of
them) go over the parapet and face death
and wounds. In a charge at the enemy
trench, such as those of the last few days, it
is even chances on death, and a very high
probability on being wounded, yet they
dash out, willingly, not of necessity only.
I never realized what to " go to their graves
like beds " meant before. And that, too, after
hours of nerve-racking shelling, with sights
and sounds round to break the hardest
nerve.

On Monday 14th we moved up towards

the trenches. Headquarters were in a village a little way back. I slept in a tiny white cottage, clean enough. A pleasant voluble woman lived there with her husband, and was proud of the fact that she had stayed in spite of shells, and even when the Germans were a bare mile off. She spoke vividly of the early October days, when a thin line of our troops were stopping the German advance, and farm carts full of wounded used to go past her house.

A report came down that evening that the Germans had forestalled us by collaring a piece of our trench. It was nothing, however—a little affair where the two lines actually touch.

Coming events made the atmosphere a little tense. Brigade Headquarters are, of course, out of the turmoil and yet responsible for it. There was a sense of unreality in having dinner in the ordinary way.

Next morning I walked up to our advanced H.Q. These were at the back of the village through which our trenches run. We had the two lowest rooms of a house, in the attics of which was an artillery observing station. We also had dug-outs in the garden, where the telephones were installed.

The house was about 1200 yards from the German lines. It had not been much shelled, being behind the ridge we occupy, though the whole of the left front could be seen from the attics.

This Brigade was to make the attack at 6 p.m. Other attacks were to take place right and left. I was using a section of machine-guns borrowed from another Brigade to enfilade German communication trenches with long range fire (1200–1700 yards). The advantage of this is :

(1) The angle of descent is steep and you drop bullets into trenches.

(2) The high trajectory takes you safely over your own advanced troops.

(3) The distance, combined with the insignificance of a machine-gun, makes it quite impossible for the enemy to find you ; you can safely come into action in the best place in the open, and can observe your own fire and the course of the action, from the guns themselves. This, of course, artillery cannot do.

At first I had thought the guns should be in the top floor of a suitable house, but it became clear that the open was much better, so I planted them down by the side of a road with a splendid view. The men could work in a ditch, and longish grass and a bush or two made them quite invisible. No protection was required.

The subaltern in charge was keen and very intelligent. I had a telephone wire from him to the H.Q. dug-out, where I sat mostly during the show, getting all the latest information and directing his fire. It is a dreadfully safe position when one thinks what is happening in front. Yet I can't imagine anyone wishing to be in front.

The rest of the machine-guns of the Brigade were left with their Regiments—those of the three Regiments in reserve being, of course, under my orders if required.

The morning went by—a hot bright morning—and the hour drew nearer. I had a pocket gardening dictionary (just the thing I have been looking for—I must send Alice one) and read about the culture of asparagus. Early in the afternoon the great bombard-

ment began, and after 5 swelled to a
tremendous din. The tension grew almost
unbearable. There in that garden, with a
mass of great cherry-coloured poppies bright
in the sun in one corner, and a white rose
tree in full bloom over the dug-out, one
thought of the men up against the front
wall of the trench—so many of them so
near the end. I rang up the guns—all was
ready. I went out on to the road to watch
the final bombardment. The line of the
trenches was covered by a cloud of dust.
Every moment a great black burst of smoke
opened and spread at some point of the
enemy's position. It was a few minutes to
six. Their high explosive shells were searching the reverse side of our ridge (where I got
into it the other day). Three minutes to—
two minutes—then a vast fan-shaped cloud
shot up on the right where our people had
prepared a mine. And they were off. I
prayed for them.

I went back to the dug-out, listening to
the rattle of the machine-guns. Then information began to come in. At first we
heard they had taken the first trench, but

it was untrue. Then a message came from
the right battalion commander that his
right was held up by machine - guns, that
his centre had got into the German trench,
that his left was held up. Then the left
battalion reported they had got to a German
trench in front of them—a mistake, I think.
The machine-guns had been switched off to
a further objective, in case our people might
have got forward. When it was clear that
they had not, I turned the guns back to the
communication trench—a new one, only dug
by the Germans a day or two before, and
presumably valuable to them. It was clear
enough now for the subaltern to see, and
he spotted the bullets falling on the parapet
on either side of the trench (which ran
directly from him), and therefore presumably
in it as well. Very soon he saw parties of
Germans leave the trench and run back
through the shelling over the open rather
than use the trench where he blocked it.

Time went very quickly. I stood outside
the dug-out or sat in it, telephoning, smoking
hard. The General, following it on a map,
ordered the artillery to bombard again the

parts of the trench we had not got. I did a good deal of talking to the Colonels in the trenches—heard them asking returned wounded men to describe events—spoke to Divisional H.Q. and got and gave information. The light failed, and we had not made good our footing. The machine-guns stopped because they could not see.

The night went by, with much planning and replanning of another attack. I got about half an hour's sleep. A fresh battalion was to try with the bayonet before dawn : but this could not be arranged in time. An attack was to take place at 5.30 ; but mist came on, and this was stopped. The afternoon was finally decided on. I dozed most of the morning in the house.

What one dared not think about was the wounded lying between the two lines. Some had been brought in, but not all. The Germans fire on any wounded man who moves.

The next attack was a repetition of the first, and had the same result. The machine-guns got additional chances. Another communication trench was reported to be full of reinforcements. I turned the guns on to it, and the artillery observer said he saw the men in the trench scatter in all directions. This was at 1200 yards. We went a little short to start with, but the troops in front telephoned to say so, and then we got in.

Again darkness came on. The machine-guns had done very well. In addition to the above they had opened on a lot of Germans standing up to shoot, and made them keep their heads down. They fired between 20,000 and 30,000 rounds in the two days. We slept heavily that night. Next day I went up into the trenches to see that the guns up there were properly disposed.

They had been subjected to a terrific German bombardment, but the parapets had been repaired during the night. Things were being cleared up. Men were lying asleep in the sun, on the floor of the trench ; those awake were quite cheery. Here and there one stepped over others who would never wake. The trenches are so narrow that removing the dead and wounded is very difficult. At one spot I looked over the parapet with a periscope, to see the field of fire of a gun. Just in front lay a man as he had fallen, his head to the enemy, knee bent, arm forward. It was a strange picture in that glass, very remote from the trench I was in—a stretch of torn, lifeless orchard, with no parapet or work visible, and just its one occupant.

I came back along the communication trench I was shelled in before. They were shelling it now, but slightly : only one came near us. We ducked to the bottom of the trench as it whistled on its way to us, and it went off with a great bang a few yards away, quite harmlessly.

I was walking down with the signal officer, who was looking to his line. I must admit I thought him horribly deliberate.

We came back to this town that evening. The Germans later started a tremendous cannonade ; it was only nerves, however.

Although no trench was taken, and losses were heavy, there is no doubt that good was done by pinning down a large number of German troops here, and a great many guns, while the French go on with their advance.

As you see, my job is a particularly safe, if not very glorious, one. It is very interesting. I am going to look after the bomb throwing too.

The Germans searched for my machine-guns, but never got near them.

LETTER 18

A Village,
23rd June, 1915.

WE have now moved here, a village about 5 miles out. We are in a fascinating house, with a pretty little garden deep in trees, and an old fountain playing into a fish-pond in the middle. When one sits there of an evening, with the low sunshine and shadows on the grass, and the great bell ringing in the church just behind, it is difficult to realize we are at war. This and the trenches seem so very far apart.

This is rather a nice old house belonging to a sort of Squire-farmer, now serving. His wife and daughter, capable and hard-working, live in another part of the house, and we have some very pleasant rooms. I sleep in the next farmhouse, in a little room with a tiled floor and a straw bed. We are a very cheerful and friendly Mess.

I have taken on the training of the grenade people, as well as machine-guns. I don't know anything about grenades, but organize the show. Of course numbers are getting more and more important. To-day the woman in whose field they drill was complaining to the officer who instructs them of the damage done. He was just assuring her that they did no damage at all, when a tree at the far end rose into the air and fell with a crash ! Some one was testing gun-cotton ; but it spoilt his argument.

G

LETTER 19

WE went into the trenches—or at least two battalions of the Brigade did—last week. We were only there a day or two, and then handed it over to a New Army Brigade.

It was not a very nice part of the line. An advance had been made there a month ago, and the result was that our front trench was not very satisfactory, and our support trench was behind an extremely unpleasant old German trench. Also the Germans paid a certain amount of attention to the place with trench mortars and shells. Luckily they thought we occupied their old trench, and often shelled that. It was really quite unoccupiable : the parapets contained such large numbers of very inadequately covered German dead.

I went round the trenches one day with the General ; and he frightened me by

keeping on getting out on the surface when
the communication trench got muddy.

" There's no danger," he said, " and besides
they never hit you first shot." However, all
was well. At the point of our salient the
German parapet was about 80 yards off.
" I suppose that's our front line parapet,"
said the General, looking over. Luckily the
Boches were having dinner (always a good
time to go round the trenches). On the last
day we were in I took the next Brigade
machine-gun officer round. Nothing much
was happening. We were worried at one
point by what is known as a " whizz-bang "
—a beastly little thing that you don't hear
coming, and that suddenly goes off with a
double explosion — and they were putting
some high explosive along another communication trench ; otherwise it was quiet.
The old German trench was not a very en-
livening thing to pass through (the waxen-
looking hand sticking out of the side of it
into the communication trench was a well-
known but not an inspiriting object), and
I liked him for the honesty with which, as
we got back through our support trench and

turned on to the road, he heaved a deep sigh and said " Thank God." It was his first visit.

We lived in a farmhouse a mile back— rather a smelly, fly-infested place, with a filthy moat round it. There were people living in the farmhouse and in the village. On the last afternoon I mounted the Uhlan without regret, and set off to ride the fifteen miles to this place.

By the way, the Uhlan is a mare that was collared from the Germans up near Ypres. I took her over with rather a bad reputation ; however now, after a succession of fights, from which we both returned very hot and drippy, we have come to a working compromise : I admit I can't get her past a steam roller without help, and she agrees to face everything else. To start with, she wouldn't face a motor at all. I rode over here with the Staff Captain —a pleasant ride, along the canal a good part of the way, through flat country and cornfields. In the evening we fetched up here.

This is simply a dream. It was a monastery up to the time of the Revolution. Then most of the buildings were knocked down, but the church (partly Norman), this house (the Priory—xvii century) and the most lovely old stone wall round the gardens, wood and orchard were left. The house and church are in a grove of great trees (limes and walnuts mostly). There is a small walled garden behind the house, a very large one next it, with fruit-tree walks ; and besides these a walled paddock, now in standing corn, with a little red-roofed chapel at the far corner, and a nut walk down one side. The house has nice panelled rooms, and belongs to three charming middle-aged French ladies, who cooked for us the first evening, before the transport turned up, and gave us a meal served with old silver spoons and forks. They work the small garden (we do a turn of digging for them occasionally), and let the big one to an old peasant and his wife and family. At least the family is now mostly at the war. " We were so happy," the wife said, " before this came. We and our three sons could work here and live comfortably. But one is a prisoner and one wounded and one in the trenches."

It is all very delightful and peaceful, after the other shows. I gather the Division will be in Reserve for a bit.

Many thanks for starting the grenade badges. They are much in request.

One can hear the guns in the distance : but muffled and far away.—just a reminder of what is going on all the time.

I see two of the ladies sitting at a table under the walnut - trees, in the shade, in front of the house, making pillows stuffed with lime-tree flowers : the church bell will start again presently (a fine-toned one ; all these villages seem to have that), and they will go across to service. The battle line seems very far away. It makes a delightful rest. On the other side the little garden lies still in the sunshine between its grey stone walls. Roses and white lilies, poppies and red currants catch the sun.

LETTER 20

28.8.15.

WE moved back into the trenches about
ten days ago. It was a bit of the line, parts
of which are anything but quiet. But by
returning two rifle grenades for every one
of the Germans we calmed them down a bit.
Walking back up one of the long communication trenches one evening I got a curious
effect. It happened that for the moment
there was no noise whatever. Looking over
the parapet, there was no sign of life or
movement or occupation at all : just acres
and acres of fallow grass and cereals, turning
brown, with an occasional scar or pile of
sandbags ; broken, bare trees ; stumps of
houses ; and a red sun sinking over all. It
seemed as if one was the last man on earth :
utterly alone in utter desolation.

I spent a night up in the trenches and
found it rather pleasant —for a change.

We lived in a very pleasant little country

house, near a great château. This was just
what one has pictured the French château
of Louis XV: a great red brick flush-
shuttered house, with its courtyard behind
containing enormous walnut - trees, and a
wood round. In front had been the lawns
and gardens —now all trampled by transport.
In the wood is an English and Indian grave-
yard. Many of the trees are barked by
horses. I should think the place had been
a bit ruinous before the war : it's very part
worn now.

I went through there last Sunday. The
Scotsmen were having a service in the
mottled shade of the wood —singing para-
phrases with fine-toned voices, if a bit
slowly. Later I heard them singing " Art
thou weary " extremely well. Then I attended the Grenade Company's Service in
front of the château. The padre, a very
good chap, popped on his surplice and cassock
almost as he jumped from his horse. His
spurs twinkled below. At his request I led
the singing ; but unfortunately differed
from the men as to one of the tunes. They
won, of course, hands down.

LETTER 21

WE are just going back for a bit, after a
week in the trenches. It is a very interesting bit of the line, and has given some
good practice to my bombers, there being
points where an exchange of bombs takes
place every night.

Very odd points they are too—the queer-
est I have yet seen. I went up one night to
see how things were being carried out. I
dined with the C.O. of the Regiment holding
that bit, and we walked up afterwards. It
was a moonlight night, and we plodded up
perhaps half a mile of communication trench
with sandbagged walls (all the trenches on
this ridge have been greatly improved since
we were here before). The jagged spike of
brickwork which is all that remains of the
village church tower stood up as a land-
mark.

After twisting and turning along the parts of different trenches that make up the route, we came at last to the local bomb store—a deep hole, cheerfully lit. Here we looked at some faulty bombs, and discussed matters with the bombing officer. Then we went on across the Sunken Road, now a stream carrying the overflow from the mine-pumps, to the bombing area.

In this part the Germans are apparently trying to fix a great gulf between us and them by exploding mines between us. At any rate there is a succession of deep craters they have made—30 to 40 feet deep and 60 feet and more across—that in places run into one another and form a sort of moat. Our people have sapped out to one edge of these—the Boches have presumably done the same on the other. In one case we have the whole crater (a small one), which now makes a redoubt.

We started at the quiet end, through a narrow opening in the old parapet—along a narrow slit in the ground—up on to a step, displacing a bomber and a sentry, and looked over a couple of sandbags.

It really was the strangest, weirdest sight
in the moonlight. A deep quiet hole, half
in shadow, half with its steep sides mistily
lit ; black lumps against the stars on the far
side—perhaps the lip of the crater, perhaps
a bit of German parapet. An odd sense of
being on the surface of the moon. An eerie
feeling that things *must* be lurking behind
those black heaps. Sometimes the tension
of the place gets so much that the bomber
has to throw a bomb—for company. There
is no wire, of course, in front of these saps :
it cannot be got out. The people in them
feel at the mercy of anything that can
creep : and it looks a place for creeping
things.

We went on, by other slits, to other sap-
heads, and came to the lively part. Here
bombs were flying. The Boches could not
quite throw into the trench ; every now and
then there was a deep thud on the parapet,
and bits of earth flew over. Our men were
hurling bombs back in what they hoped was
the right direction, you could see the
flashes of the burst against the black tumbled
edge. I don't suppose we were getting into

them though. Some of the men were enjoying it. Some, on the other hand, were
not. So back to Headquarters, and a walk
home along the canal.

LETTER 22

FOR days our shells have been flying overhead, and are now. I have been up in the trenches supervising machine-gun work — (batteries of machine-guns covering enemy communication trenches). While our people are shooting, there is a constant swishing roar going on overhead, punctuated by booms and bangs. It is rather like the noise of a heavy sea on a beach and breakwater. And looking over the parapet reminds one of the sea. There is a flat grey-green expanse, with long white lines across it, like foam-crests (these are the chalk parapets of our forward trenches), and great spouts of smoke where the rollers reach the shore — the white mounds of the German line.

Field guns, wire-cutting with shrapnel, larger guns blowing-in trenches, biggest guns removing almost acres at a time — everything has been at it.

LETTER 23

BATTALION H.Q.,
18th October, 1915.

IT is long enough now since the battle of Hulluch to sit down and write an account of it.

You remember I described the preliminary bombardment. I was in the trenches during those four days, working machine-gun fire at night on the German communication trenches opposite. We had twelve guns going all night on this job and others on their barbed wire —stopping them repairing it.

On the evening of the 24th September I went across to the gun position I intended to be with when the curtain rose. It consisted of a narrow, winding connecting trench, four good big dug-outs, and six gun positions. It really did not show from the front at all, as all the earth had been taken away in sandbags at night. It commanded

a splendid view, the ground dropping in
front, and then rising to the ridge on which
Hulluch and Loos are—bare, open ground,
seamed with chalk parapets. The high road
ran close by, into and through the German
trenches, and was planted with trees (elms
of sorts). The panorama stretched from the
Hohenzollern Redoubt to the Souchez hills.
I went across from the other position in the
evening, hoping for a bit of sleep. No such
luck—I had to spend the entire night tinker-
ing at old machine-guns and trying to make
them work.

Dawn came on, misty and damp. We
were to fire through the intensive bombardment just before the attack. At the given
hour we started.

The light was growing; and then one
noticed little wisps of white smoke at intervals along our line—close intervals. These
grew longer and spread, grew longer and
spread more, joined and formed a wall,
blotting out the other side of the valley (we
had ceased firing now). The wall grew
higher and higher, varied here and there by
darker smoke; drifted in rolls very slowly

towards the German lines; still the smoke
was pouring out of the original points. You
must imagine the wall it formed, not as a
blank mist, but as a mass of rolling curls of
smoke ; and you must picture them stretch-
ing away, mile after mile, till they merged
in the dim clouds beyond Souchez.

It was like a Doré illustration to some
scene in Hell.

We could not see the German trenches, of
course. The moment came when we knew
our infantry had started. We had had one
man killed by a stray bullet, and the other
position had two. That was just bad luck.

We peered into the cloud. The noticeable
thing was that there was hardly any answer-
ing Artillery fire. We could see our men
walking about behind our front line on the
right ; we could see our own supports
getting out of the trenches in front of us.
Then some Artillery observing officers ran
down the road, which the day before would
have been certain death. At last the cloud
had moved far enough on for us to see the
German parapet —and after a time (not at
first) I definitely saw Highlanders on it. It

was ours—but at no small cost, for Germans
had been left, sniping and machine-gunning,
up to the last.

Our work was over, and the guns went to
join their battalions.

Our Brigade was in support, and the Regiments were then moving up the communication trenches. I went a little way back
up the road, and found Brigade Headquarters in some trenches there.

As I got back to H.Q. the horse guns were
coming into action. They looked splendid :
three batteries galloped down the slope over
the grass—unlimbered—their teams galloped
back, and the guns started firing. After
all these months of sitting behind barbed
wire it made a lump rise in one's throat.

Our Brigade had been committed by now,
and had gone forward in support of the
leading Brigades. Two of our battalions
were over the first Boche trench and getting
forward under very heavy rifle fire. But we
could not see that. By this time some
strings of German prisoners were coming
along the road : and I went over to them.
They were a quite unremarkable lot—

H

mostly rather undersized —one or two school-masters among them.   They were smoking, several of them, large Dutch pipes.   The escort provided the matches.   When asked about our gas, they said " It had a nasty smell ! "   They were very anxious to answer questions, and produced their books and papers on the slightest provocation.   I rather fancy they were glad to be alive.   They were Reservists.   One Tommy, limping along behind, was singing, vaguely and generally, " Shoot the ——s," but otherwise no one was bothering about them.

A little later the General and I walked up the road towards the front line.   Before that I had established an advanced bomb store in the German front line.

The space between our lines and theirs was not a place to remember.   I don't mean at all that the whole of it was full of casualties, for the greater part of it was empty. But there were more than enough to make one glad to forget it.   I felt as I looked at them that it was not *our* success but *theirs :* for they had paid for it.

The General and I went on up the road to

a trench near our front line. Having looked around, we came back again. I persuaded him not to stand on the top of the old Boche parapet, talking to people in the trench. There was a fairly continuous whistle of " overs."

There was not much incident during the afternoon, except rather a surprising number of people drifting back from away on our left flank.

That night the General told me to go and get some sleep. I was very short of sleep and glad to do it. He and the Brigade Major were up near the front line during the night, and contributed largely to rallying a slight set-back produced by a Boche counter attack, meant to recover their guns, of which eight were in our hands, not yet removed to the rear. The counter attack was utterly broken in the end by a brilliant bayonet charge.

I slept heavily in the shell-proof shelter of our rear Headquarters.

There is not much to record of the next few days. Our Brigade was left to hold the captured trenches, the remains of the leading Brigades being withdrawn. The Germans had developed a very strong bomb attack ; and we were at a considerable disadvantage in regard to the bomb provided for us, but our bomb training worked out all right. I was mostly occupied in pushing bombs up so as to keep the trenches supplied.

Life was not without its little interests. Up in the bomb store in the village in rear one morning, I was talking to a Divisional Major, and had just said " We may as well talk in safety " and turned down into the cellar where the bombs were, when an H.E. landed in a shed the other side of the yard, and filled the air with bricks and tiles. The same afternoon I was walking down the road. One hears shells coming and almost at once knows which side of one they are coming. Well, several small ones had landed comfortable distances off, and another was heard on its way ; and I realized with acute discomfort that this wasn't going either side, but was coming straight at me. I hunched up my shoulders, and the thing burst on the road about 10 yards behind me.

It was a small H.E. without shrapnel, and did no harm whatever.

By the 30th September the men were getting pretty tired. It was the sixth day of more or less anxious work in the new trenches, the first day having been a severe fight. Somebody was pretty badly shelled every day. In the battalion holding the left that night the only senior officer left was a Major, a very good man.

We (Brigade Headquarters) were in the old trenches half a mile back. After dinner that evening messages began to come back that the Boches had broken into our line, but at first they were vague ; then, about 11 o'clock, particulars began to come in. It seemed that they had rushed a post in the centre with bombers. They then tried to spread in both directions, but did not succeed in doing this : as on both sides our men formed bombers' " blocks " in the trench. The Boches got two gun-pits.

The Brigadier, the Brigade Major and I hung about one end of the telephone all through the night. It was very thrilling— rather like playing chess by telegraph for great issues. The telephones were in a very deep dug-out, 15 feet down. There we sat on boxes, with 8 or 10 signallers and a couple of candles, smoking hard. From time to time I went out to try and hurry up the supply of bombs—they were running short. An idiot sergeant at the bomb store behind delayed matters because, he said, he had orders not to issue without special instructions. At last the bomb carts came up the road and I sent them on at a gallop. They had 10 bombs left at the crucial point when the new stream began to arrive. There would have been no hitch but for the sergeant : still the consumption was much greater than one had thought possible. " Bombs and matches "—the Major on the left had anxiously asked me over the telephone when they would arrive. Meantime in the dug-out we were trying to devise plans to retake the gun-pits. We were talking to all three battalions—the two in the line and the one in support. The Boches soon had machine - guns up. They were delivering constant and heavy bomb attacks in both directions. It says much for our people that they did not get another yard.

The left battalion tried a counter bomb attack, and cleared the Boches back a bit : but, mainly owing to the type of bomb supplied us, they could make no more progress, and in the end fell back again. The Boche had a very good bomb indeed, which enabled him to throw about three to one.

In the dug-out we were drawing plans on bits of paper and racking our brains for another move that would recover the trench. Gradually it became evident that dawn would be on us without our having done it : and orders were given to fill the trench in at the ends of the parts held.

At about 5.30 a.m. the Brigadier said one of us had better get some sleep, and sent me off to the mess dug-out to do so. I went there, sat in a chair, dropped off, and — before 6 the door opened and there was the Brigadier. " I've a job for you," he said. " The C.O. on the left is killed and you must go up there and take over." I think I got there about 7.

As you see, the position was a little bit

dicky. The men were thoroughly done up. The end of the trench was practically sticking out into Bocheland, without any wire to cover it either. The trench was also liable to be cut in half if an attack down a sap there was successful. I did not much expect that ; though it seemed quite likely that the Boches (who were clearly strong, and good fresh troops) would try and expand from the captured point. It was also on the cards that we might be told to go and retake the thing—I had no doubts as to the result of that.

I went first to the H.Q. dug-out, a big comfortable German cavern, with names written over the walls. There I found the very young adjutant (there was not an officer in the trench who had served before the war). Then I went up to take stock of my command.

. . . . .

It may amuse you to know that the comment of one of the subalterns, in talking it over afterwards, was " You looked so cheery " —and honestly I did my best to. The men were thoroughly done up—tired, very dirty,

of course, worn by a very great strain on the
top of a more or less continuous week of it
(I don't think many of the officers had expected to keep the trench through the
night). Yet they responded wonderfully :
I think what struck me more than anything else was the way they had bucked up
again by the afternoon (it was a fine day).
In the morning they seemed, many of them,
worn out, with a general air of expecting
something unpleasant. By the afternoon
they were very much alive and thirsting for
the blood of the Boche. They are splendid
people.

The Germans were sniping with amazing
accuracy at about 100 yards range. The
Major had been killed that way, as he
directed the filling in, in the dawn. The
parapet of the trench was not too good :
one had to be careful. A subaltern I was
talking to got a bullet across his cap—it
left a burned mark on the cloth.

The first thing to do was to make the
rather flimsy block at the end secure; then
to take stock of ammunition and bombs,
arrange the bombers, and strengthen the

dangerous end. By the middle of the morning, all being still quiet, I felt pretty secure, and so reported.

I had expected at least to get shelled, but even that did not happen. We got the welcome news we were to be relieved that night, but the relieving party was first to take the gun-pits! which seemed a quaint idea, and did not, as a matter of fact, come off. We stood by to help the proposed attack, but nothing happened except the usual brilliant illumination by the Boche, and we got out by midnight. When all were out, I walked up that familiar, fateful road for the last time. The quiet figures one had passed and repassed so often that the road seemed dedicate to them were no longer there. Time had been found to lay them deep in that shrouding dust to which they had returned.

We trekked through the night (I practically fell asleep in the saddle) and fetched up at a little village after sunrise. There we slept—heavily.

We had two days out, in which I began to get in touch with the battalion, and then

moved up into trenches more to the left.
Here we remained for a week, without much
incident. The most exciting moment for
me was one night when I went out to look
at our wire, with a view to further work on
it. The officer commanding the company
and his sergeant were with me. I had said,
rather grandly, " Oh, they never see you
in those Verey lights if only you stay still."
We were at the wire, 150 yards from the
Germans, and I was talking about it (rather
too loudly, perhaps) ; one or two lights had
come over, and one fell behind us ; suddenly
there really was a hail of bullets and a
bouquet of lights : ten or twenty men had
opened rapid fire on us. I thought no more
about " standing still," but lay very flat on
my front ; and, when they stopped, scuttled
back to the parapet, hoping they wouldn't
send up another light as I was getting over.
None of us were hit.

We came out of the trenches at last, and
the next day were told that there was to be
a big attack on the right, and that, if the gas
acted, we were to go across and take the
German trenches opposite. We stood by

ready to move : but the wind was un-
favourable.

Then we moved really back and are now
here—a very pretty village behind Béthune.
We were to have had ten days (half our
strength is draft), but ten minutes ago we
got an order to move back to the trenches
at once. So off we go again.

I gather this job will not last very long ;
meanwhile it is very interesting.

LETTER 24

I am shortly going to hand over the battalion to a C.O. belonging to the Regiment itself, who has just come out from England. I shall be sorry to part with them—we have got on very well together, and they are a fine lot.

Last week they took some craters in front of this place in grand style. They went over the top in the middle of the afternoon (no mean performance in itself on this much-disputed ridge) at very short notice, as it was thought the Boches were getting on too fast with their mining. As a result three new craters are in our hands.

In a few days now I shall be back at Brigade H.Q.

LETTER 25

THERE are not many events to record : on the contrary, everything has been very pleasantly peaceful.

We moved down to the Amiens district, and I was busy for a fortnight in December, living at Brigade H.Q. in an old château and riding over nearly every day on the Uhlan to the Brigade Grenade School. It was a pleasant 4 or 5 mile ride, on nice days, up on to the uplands by curious small valleys with sides like embankments (glacier beds, I should think) and across to the big farm where my 150 learners and 10 officers were. The people of that farm (a lonely one at the end of a long row of pine trees) were all deaf, and at first surly, but afterwards thawed. The officers were a cheery little party, and the class got on well.

The Brigade was to move to a new Kitchener Division the week before Christmas. I pushed off to Amiens for the Sunday of the move—having no particular job to do.

There is a little railway line with a *halte* near the château, and an Amiens train was reputed to go at 6 p.m. I got to the shed by the line before 6, and at 7 a train turned up going the other way. However, a farmer who had arrived a quarter of an hour before told me I might still hope. He told me a lot of other things—how the owner of the château had the biggest estate in Picardy, he and his wife ; how people had not sown last year, for fear of the Germans reaping ; how good his bit of ground was, growing corn even 6 feet high if you manured it — and various other homely details. He met his wife, shook me warmly by the hand, and I was left again to the little dark shed and the moonlight on the wide fields and woods. At last my train came, and soon I found myself established in a nice hotel in Amiens, enjoying an excellent dinner.

The waiter was a joy. He was exactly like the French waiter of comedy, or rather

farce. He had square flat feet and long
whiskers. He plodded about, made wonderful faces, and took a paternal interest in
every one.

I woke to a jolly morning, hot rolls and
coffee. It is a real French town—very
different from English Béthune—and the
passers-by were French soldiers in blue
greatcoats and helmets, and neat French-
women. I went to the Cathedral, and found
it very beautiful. The great doorways are
all sandbagged up. Service was going on,
impressive as always, with a large congregation, and many Canons in ermine tippets.
In the afternoon I heard one of them preach-
ing in the nave. He preached well, though
of course I couldn't understand a lot of it.
It was on charity, and the way he said,
almost softly, very musically, as good French
always sounds, " J'avais faim et *vous*—vous
m'avez donné à manger "—struck me very
much.

I did some shopping (Madame of the boot-
shop sold me some of her own soap because
she thought the other shops would be shut.
" It's all right," she said, as she produced

half a new cake that looked like carbolic,
" I use it for my face ") ; then took a walk
over the many streams of Amiens, and so
back to dinner and bed.

I motored out next day to the Brigade in
its new quarters : and almost at once was
called for by the Division to start a Divisional Grenade School. They seemed surprised that we were ready to start their
school on so large a scale and at once, but
there were only 10 days before the first of
the new lot went into the trenches, and we
were accustomed to starting Grenade Schools
on nothing but an exercise book. The great
thing was to get something going, so I
got them to order in 200 men and 12 officers
the next day. The staff officers left me and
one of my grenade officers with some mis-
givings. I don't think they even believed
we could get billets for the men without an
interpreter ; and they said the inhabitants
of the selected village were " unfriendly."
As a matter of fact, we had no trouble at
all, and by the next evening the whole
thing was going.

Since then we have been working hard (I

I

wouldn't let them go back to their Regiments for Christmas, except for the day), and are just completing the second 200. I have got a dozen N.C.O.'s as instructors from our old Regiments, who tell the men yarns about actual bombing and interest them thoroughly; my Sergeant-Major is a fine chap and almost an orator. He gives them excellent advice in very broad Scotch. The other day I came upon him as he was addressing a squad, who were listening open-mouthed. "Ye've been here a week," he was saying, "and some of ye are good bombers, and some of ye are bad bombers, and some of ye are *faur-r-r* worse than that."

The men are all Kitcheners, and have been training in England for 15 months. So that I think it is a real relief to them to come up against experience instead of theory, and feel themselves in touch with the actuality that they have been playing at so long. They'll have enough of it before they've done. They are very keen and intelligent, and get on quickly.

In a day or two we move up nearer the front and continue these classes.

Later on I shall return to the Brigade to take over the Machine-Gun Company which will be formed. Sixteen machine-guns is not a bad command—I mean to get back on leave first.

By the way, we had a practice attack one day with the bombers wearing the new steel helmets and the leather jerkins (loose sleeveless coats) that are now issued. The effect was extraordinarily Japanese.

LETTER 26

WE left the village from which I last wrote,
and moved here, where grenade work is in
full swing again. This is a pleasant part of
the country. The river winds among its
marshes round steep headlands, on the top
of which are well-tilled plateaux and some
woods. A few fields are left fallow, but not
many. The farmers' wives and daughters
are doing a large part of the work.

One gets to know these villages very inti-
mately, living in people's houses and seeing
their life from within. There are many little
places in France that I know far more about
than I do about any similar place in England.
One drops into the middle of a village, shares
the quarters of some small farmer, and goes
into the homes of most of the other village
worthies, with whom one's officers or men are

116

billeted. You get on better with them, too, if you take an interest in them.

I will try and give you an idea of what the people were like at our last place.

.   .   .   .   .

Old Madame Bouton sat most of the day in the chimney corner in her little room with the red-tiled floor. There was no fire on the hearth : the fire burned in a sort of iron vase that stuck out into the room, and was connected to the chimney by an iron oven.

Madame Bouton had a little table beside her with her prayer book on it. Sometimes she was reading, sometimes talking to a crony who had dropped in, and sometimes (especially after dusk) doing nothing. Madame Bouton was seventy-five, but she had received us cheerfully when we came to ask her for her other sitting-room as an orderly room, and at once began to remove the nineteen plants in pots from the window.

" We hope we don't put you out very much," we said.

" It is war," she answered, with a smile and a shrug of her shoulders. She did

object, however, on the second day, when
the doctor saw the sick in the orderly room.
Ten men tramped through her kitchen, one
after another, in and out, and finally the
doctor demanded hot water and towels.

" It is too much for anyone of my age,"
she said, and threatened to go off once more
into a description of her husband's decease,
which, it appeared, had taken place fifteen
years ago, suddenly. However, we promised
that she should not be disturbed in this way
again.

Very different had been Madame Delville,
who, indeed, had sent us on to Madame
Bouton.

" She has a room that will do for an
office," said Madame Delville. " I can't
possibly spare you this one." The room in
question contained two chairs, a bicycle,
and some clothes ; the house was a large
one, and the evening before we had been
half promised the use of the room. " I
don't care," she said, coming through the
parlour from the kitchen, where she was
doing her hair, " I might want to use the
room any time."

Madame Delville was short and substantial; two locks of dark hair were tied under her chin, while her hands were busy with the rest; and she looked at us over this collar of hair in so determined a manner that we gave up the attempt.

Madame Sévigné, of the farm on the other side of the river, was most helpful from the first. Yes, she had plenty of room in her lofts; and she showed us good, dry barns half full of straw, that any platoon might be glad of. She could take in officers too; it was true that Grandfather called out at night sometimes—perhaps for five minutes, perhaps for an hour. But if they had been told about it they would understand. Grandfather stopped calling out for good and all a few days later, and we saw the little procession come to the church. First two little boys in white, one carrying a cross, the other a brush; then the village carpenter, intoning the sentences. He also had a sort of surplice on. Then the old curé; and then the coffin, covered with a white sheet. The Army Service Corps repair shop established in the church porch stopped working as the

procession came along, and an officer saluted;
the curé took the brush and sprinkled coffin
and mourners, and then all passed into the
church.

We did not see much of the curé, who
served two or three villages. He was a
kindly-looking, grey-haired man, and used
to plod up the village street in enormous
boots, holding up the skirts of his cassock
behind him out of the ankle-deep mud.

On Christmas Day in the afternoon I saw
him kneeling at the Altar, while six of the
village boys knelt in a row behind him and
one swung a censer. The joiner and a
farmer were chanting the service in fine rich
voices, from lecterns on either side of the
little Manger group that had been arranged
on a table at the chancel step. On each
lectern was a very large service book, and
both men wore copes. The congregation
was not large; and Madame Cailleux, at
whose house we had our Mess, regretted the
decay of church attendance.

" Would you believe it ? " she said. " The
schoolmaster punishes the children who are
late for school, even though it is because

they went to Mass ! And some of the other
children tell my girl that it is *sottise* on
my part to send her to Catechism. But I
don't know how a girl can do without being
taught to pray."

Madame Cailleux has a daughter of ten,
and a pretty little fair-haired boy. Her
husband is a prisoner. She comes from
Boulogne, and finds the country "*triste.*"
One of the many doors out of our mess-room
opens into the children's room ; and every
evening about dinner-time she brings them
through on their way to bed, and the boy
kisses his hand to us. She has had an
officers' mess in her house for some months,
and likes the company it provides.

Just over the bridge there is a large room
that was an *estaminet,* years ago ; and in
the little house attached to it lives M. Leroy.
A platoon is billeted in the room ; M. Leroy,
however, appears to be totally unconcerned.
He is an old man, with dreamy eyes and a
small far-away voice which it is extremely
difficult to catch. He seems as though he
had been shut up at the same time as the
estaminet, and, like it, is falling into dis-

repair. But there is nothing vague or uncertain about the bill for damages that he presents as our stay draws to an end. There it is—a detailed list, written out in a strong, clear hand, with the name of the Regiment (wrong, however) and the date of its arrival. If the platoon had spent their whole time, working with all available tools, they could hardly have got through the job ; and, if the *estaminet* had been a spick-and-span going concern, the damage could hardly have been greater. Oak beams six inches square are reported to have been cut up and taken away ; walls, windows, cupboards have been broken down; the fireplace (a mere hole in the wall) has suffered " *dégât*." The old gentleman's Sunday clothes have gone, and a mattress has been damaged — and he points to a rent in a dirty old spring mattress lying in a corner of the room. As to the mattress, there is clear evidence that a cat was chased out of its interior, where it made its home, the evening we arrived ; as to the rest, we pay him a few francs for the bundles of firewood that were actually used at Christmas time. He takes the pay-

ment, satisfied apparently, and relapses into
vagueness : but no doubt presents the bill
again to the next comer.

M. Bertout, on the other hand, is a substantial farmer, short and dark, with small,
beady eyes. His great old barns hold a
company. He is quite easy and pleasant to
deal with—it is a question of "*confiance*"
between us, he says, when he claims for a
gate that he says is missing—but with
Madame one has to mind one's P's and Q's.
The day we came in she came sailing across
the farmyard as the men filed through the
barn door, her arms folded before her, a look
of pitying surprise on her face. " But it is
impossible," she said, " all those men cannot
by any means get in there." But they got in.

The next day I was taken into the barn
to see two small holes that had undoubtedly
developed in the floor. Madame pointed out
that, *of course*, the weight of so many men
was too much for the floor ; and in the cellar
below we were shown two stones that had
fallen out of the vaulting and broken some
wine bottles. The fall of the stones had, of
course, nothing to do with the weight above :

they were probably shaken out, being neither
keyed in by their shape nor cemented, but
stuck in with the local mud-plaster some
hundreds of years ago. We agreed to have
them replaced by the R.E., and to pay for
the wine, on condition the rest was moved
away.

Two days later Madame was again waiting
for us, arms more tightly folded than ever,
head erect, and smile most bellicose. Was
it to be believed ? The " *ingénieurs* " had
indeed put the stones in again—but with
cement ? No, no—with *mud !* Was such a
thing ever heard of ? We had no time that
afternoon, so, asking Madame to meet us
there two hundred years hence, when we
should find the stones still in position, we
moved on.

My sleeping billets were with the Mayor, a
comfortable-looking, pleasant man, farming
a large part of the surrounding land, and
owning the best house in the village. We
passed each other with innumerable small
courtesies whenever we met in his rooms or
passages. The Mayoress, comfortable-looking too, was of a different class from our

other hostesses ; true, she did her own cooking with the help of a maid, but she had a certain air of distinction that accorded with her position. Her hair was always arranged with some elaboration, and she was to be found of an evening in the one private sitting-room that remained to them, dressed with a certain quiet style. She always welcomed us in there, and was ready for a talk ; but it always came back to speculation as to when the war would end. " Have you heard anything fresh ? " she would ask, " When do *you* think the war will end ? " — as if it would comfort her merely to hear some one say they thought the end in sight.

But we could not rise to such heights of mendacity even for politeness' sake ; and if the Mayor was there he would shake his head and dismiss the subject with a sigh.

LETTER 27

All is still pretty peaceful here, and two glorious spring days have added to the peaceful aspect.

This afternoon I rode the Uhlan up on to the ridge east of this, and got a wonderful panorama of the line. It was a hot, sunny afternoon and very clear. The larks were singing hard. The country does not fall again, but stretches away, undulating, with dark masses of wood at intervals. One saw 6 or 7 miles in most directions—brown sweeping tracts of country that reminded one oddly of the veld. There is the same absence of detail, for of course the fields are not tilled. The woods, with their clearly defined geometrical edges, were almost the only incident.

Here and there one could trace the white

126

scars of the trenches of one side or the other.
A puff of smoke and later a dull report
showed where some spasmodic shelling was
going on, but did not disturb the stillness.
The line curves so here that on one side
the trenches disappeared 6 or 7 miles
away on the left front, on the other they
were behind one's right shoulder. The great
main roads with their lines of trees cut across
the map into the German territory. Half a
dozen woods were full of Germans ; two or
three others were our side of the line. It
gave one a slight sense of the immensity of
the thing —for this great view was only a
small extract from the Western line.

This afternoon some refugees came in from
further forward. An old woman, very calm
and collected, came up to the Orderly Room
steps and asked a man standing there if this
was the house of M. Leroux. She carried a
large hanging lamp with a big white shade
in one hand and a basket full of oddments
in the other. In the road outside was a cart
containing mattresses, a kitchen stove, chairs
hung around from odd corners, and other
household goods. I came to the rescue, and

she explained that she had had to leave her house, as 60 shells arrived yesterday; it really was too near the front—and she named a wood almost in the support line. She was quite apologetic about it, and not in the least upset. I saw her a little later, unloading at a house further down. Then I passed another younger woman coming along in floods of tears.

LETTER 28

H.Q. MACHINE-GUN COMPANY,
18.4.16.

It's just a month since I left the Grenade
School. I was sorry to leave at the time,
but felt that the show could run itself. The
Sergeant-Major said it was a pity I was
going after building it up ; but, as I told
him, that is when the builders depart. We
were a very happy little party.

The School moved one morning, with
Divisional H.Q. ; and in the afternoon I
walked across to the next village, where this
Company was. I strolled along the hills
above the river, feeling like the space between the end of one chapter and the beginning of the next.

The Company had just been collected from
the line, and the work of pulling it together
began. It consisted of the Machine-Gun
Sections of the four old Regiments of the

Brigade : of course I had had a good deal to do with them as Brigade Machine - Gun Officer. They were all very sick at leaving their own battalions and rather distrustful of each other. I told them to start with that I didn't want them to forget their old Regiments, but to start a fresh interest and pride in the company : and I think that is what is happening. The officers are a particularly nice lot, and get on well together. It has been extremely interesting ; the way of working it shapes itself as we go along, for there are no precedents.

We came right back to this little country town. The Somme runs through it and round the base of a bluff, on which are the ruined castle and the church. We have had a fortnight of glorious weather. Behind our billet is a steep hill-side, with patches of garden among nut and other trees ; and these have been growing green very deliciously. We do our work up on the high ground, with enormous stretches of country in all directions ; and sometimes in the evening we have a company concert, borrowing a piano from the *estaminet*.

I came up to the gun-shed the morning
after one of these concerts ; an enormous
volume of sound was coming out of the door
as they sang (rather well) " The Sunshine of
your Smile." Looking in, they were all as
busy as bees.

One night a concert party was performing
in the town, including a French lady from
Paris ; and to hear her put hatred of
Germany into a song with the refrain " Il y
a des corbeaux dans les villes," and describe
the fate of the " corbeaux " was absolutely
thrilling.

LETTER 29

H.Q. M.G. Coy.,
May 8th, 1916.

HERE we are in the line, after a long spell out.
These guns came out in March. Much as I
dislike anything in the way of being shelled
or sniped, there is a certain satisfaction
in being in touch with the real business
again.

This is a picturesque little market town
three miles behind the trenches. An old
stone church stands high on one side of the
cobbled *place,* and red-roofed houses straggle
down to the river and up the sides of the hill.
The town has been very little shelled, but
enough to drive away the inhabitants, so that
it is absolutely full of khaki. None of the
houses are empty and you never see civilians.

The line is a curious wavy piece, up and
down the slopes of the downs. The breadth
of the " racecourse " varies from 30 yards to

600. It is fairly quiet at present. The hilly
ground makes it possible to see great stretches
of it at a time, laid out like a map.·

The trenches lie in a village and a wood ;
and grass, nettles and thistles grow very
high along their edges. I have seen thistles
six feet high. It makes one feel like Alice in
Wonderland when she grew small —your head
is about the level of the roots of the grass,
and you go along looking up from that
position at these great plants that you are
accustomed to brush aside with your foot.
One seems to have become an insect.

I was walking round the town the other
evening. The low sun lit the square church
tower, with its clock (which is kept going,
and strikes too). A big crowd of men in
the *place* below were clustered round a shop
—now a Divisional Canteen. In a street
near the drums and fifes of a regiment were
playing Retreat. In another street I heard
a band, and found, in the courtyard of a
large billet, my old friends whom I went to
in 1914. They have started their regimental
band again, and it plays to them every afternoon while they are out of trenches. There

are no officers and very few men who were
there when I was with them.

We had a burst of magnificent weather
before we left the back area. Lilac, chest-
nut and fruit blossom came out ; the woods
covered themselves in lovely greens. We
held our company sports—picnicked for the
day in a valley a little way out of the town.
We had a couple of barrels of beer for the
men, and brought their rations out and
cooked their tea. We had football matches
(6 a side) and races and the usual pro-
gramme. We had an officers' race—100
yards— and I *nearly won !* But then I had
fifteen yards start—a yard for a year's
service ; I came in second. It was a lovely
day, and the men lay about the sides of the
valley and enjoyed themselves.

An officer's horse broke loose and galloped
off during the afternoon, and as it hadn't
turned up I went out at cockcrow to try
and spot it. It was another glorious morning, and I made my way along the woodland
and over the fields to the next village. There
I fetched up at a large farm—a manor house,
in fact—standing among big trees.

I walked into the big yard. An old lady in a close-fitting white cap and spectacles was leaning out of the kitchen window talking to an old man. They took great interest in the horse (remarking that I was very " *matinal* ") and said we must all help each other. Then the old lady asked me into the kitchen while she made me a hot drink for my cold (I had a bad one).

The kitchen had a fireplace in it about the size of your hall—blocked up now, though, with a vast iron stove. She lit some twigs in this, and heated up some milk while she talked. She made a most excellent drink, with a lot of brandy and sugar in it ; and clattered round the room in her wooden clogs, dusting and talking at the same time.

She was large and rather rheumatic, with an extremely kindly, wise old face. It seemed that she and the old man were the owners of the place. She spoke drearily of the war, and of how hard it was to farm without the men—grandfather and a boy did most of the work. She showed the usual (and natural) hatred of the Boche. She asked me if I was married, and said, like the people in the Sorcerer, that a man wanted some one to look after him in his old age. We parted with mutual expressions of esteem, and she said I was " *bon homme.*"

That afternoon we had a horse show in the same valley (we have over fifty mules and horses). The missing charger had turned up.

Next day we packed for the move. I went to pay a bill at the paint shop. The little old man was sitting in his kitchen and office, in velveteen clothes that looked much too big for him. His wife came in to assist, and they began talking about their son, killed on the Marne. They produced his photograph, which the little old lady kissed, and the photos of his wife and children (" Ah ! qu'ils sont des amours "), and said how like him the boy was. It was all rather touching —over a bill for paint !

LETTER 30

H.Q., MACHINE-GUN COMPANY,
16th June, 1916.

WE had a fairly quiet time in the trenches, and are now in the back area again, training —very close to where we were before.

Just before we came out we got the news of the battle of Jutland. As I walked back from the line one evening I saw the headline in a copy of the *Daily Mail* that some one was reading, and naturally became much excited.

Next day every one in the trenches was going about with faces about a yard long. I couldn't in the least see why : it is obvious that you can't have a big naval scrap without losing ships, and if they've done their job it's well worth it. It was partly due to the very pessimistic, not to say panicky, tone of the leaders in the papers, I think.

Our last march on the way out was over

twenty miles, which we did without a man
falling out. We halted for midday at a
village ; as we had started early we arrived
there about 9. It was Sunday, and a service
was going on —First Communion for a lot of
little boys in black suits with white bows on
their arms, and little girls in full and long
white dresses and veils and wreaths. It was
a nice old church, and all very pretty and
unaffected. Afterwards they came out, the
children in procession with the curé in
front, and then the elders of the village in
black coats and toppers. The little girls re-
appeared from the church-house and were
kissed by the grown-ups. Very sweet some
of them looked, with their fair hair brushed
back and their white finery.

A curious sight, literally pastoral, is to be
seen in this village, morning and evening.
An old shepherd in a long blue cloak with
a cape, leaning on a crook, shuffles by with
his flock behind him. From time to time he
plays on a pipe—he has two, made by himself, of horn, slung round his neck. The
sheep follow through the streets, watched,
without any fuss, by two or three dogs. The

whole group seems to have dropped out of a story book.

To-morrow, at 4 a.m. we set out on a twenty-mile trek back again.

. . . . .

P.S. —The shepherd *is* out of a fairy story : there can be no doubt about it. Just now he was bringing back the sheep, which belong to different people in the village. As the flock passed a lane leading up to one of the farms, he, without turning round, or making any other sound, just blew a few weird notes on his pipe—the sort of thing Pan played in the reeds, I should think. Whereupon a little knot of sheep obediently detached themselves from the flock, turned up the lane and went home.

LETTER 31

H.Q., M.G. Coy.,
26.6.16.

I THINK I will describe yesterday. By the time you get this the curtain will have lifted.

I spent the morning here in this little town where my H.Q. are, though some of my guns are up in the line. Our billet (lately an *estaminet*) has a little court at the back, smothered in roses—standards in the yard, ramblers growing over the iron railings and arched over the gate. Behind again is the garden, tended till a week or two ago, and at the bottom of the garden is the river. This is very like the Upper Thames—flat meadows or marshes on each side, bordered by steep- ish hills, the edges of the high ground, round which the river bends. Opposite us are clumps of willows to the water's edge. Among these a French band practises, and plays extremely well too.

It was a jolly morning, and the band was playing cheerfully. The water slipped along, unaffected by impending events, and swallows skimmed its surface. A great many mules were brought to the watering-place alongside our garden ; there was a certain amount of bustle which, with the band, rather gave the impression of Flower Show day in a country town.

But the 13 observation balloons that one could see from our doorstep would have been hard to explain. Also through our garden and all the other back gardens of the street runs a tramway the French have just made ; a funny little engine comes puffing along it from time to time.

In the afternoon I rode up to the trenches. One goes over a big ridge, and drops into a valley behind the line.

There was a good deal of noise going on, for it was the first day of the bombardment. We are in a salient here ; and on this ridge the trenches surround you to the extent of literally two-thirds of the horizon, at distances of from two miles to six. The German lines on the French side were marked by a continuous line of white and black smoke where the shells were bursting. The rest were not in sight.

Dropping down into the valley, I left the horses and walked on. The din here was incessant. Guns seemed stowed away in every clump of bush, and shells stacked everywhere. Every now and then a big thing would sail across the valley overhead with a humming rush—its parent gun too far back for the discharge to be heard. The Boche was making no reply.

I got out of the valley, on to the last ridge, in front of which our trenches lie—beyond the poplar-walled road along the top. In front was a German observation balloon. As I was walking across, I idly noticed a little white cloud to one side of the balloon. Then I saw a spark at the base of the cloud; then a flame; then the balloon began to drop, and as it dropped the flame grew and the pace increased until, one vast sheet of flame, it rushed out of sight, and a thin column of smoke was left. I believe it and another were destroyed by our aeroplanes. There were none left up.

I got to Brigade H.Q. —a series of trenches and dug-outs in a copse behind the road. There I got some instructions and a drink, and went on to our preliminary positions.

It was then dusk, and as it got darker the scene was very weird. There were heavy clouds, and under them a red band of sunset in the N.W. The continuous flashes of the guns played on the clouds like summer lightning, while over the German trenches the shrapnel was bursting in white flares, the H.E. in dull red glows. The Germans were sending up a few Verey lights : these, in more than a semicircle round us, served to show the great curve in the line. Our shells whistled overhead, and, as it got darker still, showed as red shooting stars whizzing across. We opened with two machine-guns. The noise of a stream of machine-gun bullets is like waves on a stony beach—a prolonged swish. The biggest noise was the earthquake crashing of the French trench mortars.

I left in the early morning and walked back here. You have to go carefully, for guns are everywhere, and (owing to the salient) pointing in all directions. A figure stepped out of the shadow of a little combe I was walking up. " Ne passez pas au front des pièces " it said—and I saw by my hand the muzzle of a 75.

It was too dark to see the reds, the yellows and the mauves of poppy, mustard and corn-flower with which the last ridge is covered, where the fields were tilled not long since ; but the birds were waking up, and the smell of the privet by the road and that almost pungent smell of earth in early morning grew stronger with the beginning of dawn.

.   .   .   .   .

I forgot to add to the mixture of sounds up at the front (by day at least) the excited chattering of the magpies in the copses—not continuous, but definitely in protest against particular explosions.

LETTER 32

12th July, 1916.

WHEN last I wrote, we were doing night firing on the German lines during the preliminary bombardment. The latter certainly was terrific. A German officer, being taken through our lines one day, spoke to my Sergeant-Major. The Sergeant-Major said that at that moment our men were being badly shelled in the wood. " Bombardment ? " said the German. " *You* don't know what bombardment is. We've never given you anything like what we're getting." A French officer, watching the opening of the fight from our rear positions, said it was more than he had ever seen at Verdun.

The opening day was deferred owing to the weather. On the afternoon of June 30th I rode up from the town following the gun teams, who had already started for the assembly trenches.

The river and rose gardens looked very jolly. By way of a cheerful send-off, a gramophone in one of the houses I passed was playing the Dead March in "Saul"!

I passed the night in the dug-outs we had made on the ridge overlooking the Boche lines, by our night-firing position. We had three guns going a great part of the night. The three officers who were going forward with me slept there too, when they had packed their men away ready for the start.

Word came round that the start was to be at 7.30 a.m. Soon after five I was out, looking round. The sky was clear, and so was our ridge, but the lower ground where the British and German trenches were was hidden in a sea of white mist. The sun was just topping the mist and catching the dewdrops on the grass and thistles round us. The stakes of the barbed wire round our work threw long shadows towards us. The guns were blazing away; and great black mushrooms were shooting up out of the surface of the white sea in front as the big shells burst in the German trenches. It was a strange scene—we stood about on the grass round our positions, apparently alone in the world on this brilliant morning, only disturbed by the crashing of the guns behind and the weird upheavals in the mist surface.

We stood about a little too long, a chance German bullet getting two of my men—one very slightly.

At 7 the intense bombardment began, and our machine-guns opened again on the German communication trenches. The mist was clearing off. The officers had joined their sections, and I went forward with two orderlies to the H.Q. of the supporting battalion, which were to be my H.Q. also.

There was a wonderful air of cheery expectancy over the troops. They were in the highest spirits, and full of confidence. I have never known quite the same universal feeling of cheerful eagerness.

The moment came, and they were all walking over the top, as steadily as on parade, the tin discs on their backs (to show the guns where they were) glittering in the sun. I was some way behind the front line, and watched the supporting troops marching forward. I could not see the " racecourse."

Very soon German prisoners began to come back, and we could see our leading lines topping the German support lines.

Our Brigade was to take and hold the trenches and redoubt opposite us, and then another Brigade was to go through, half left, and take an important village (all this was accomplished up to time, though the fact that the Division on our left was held up for a bit hampered us a good deal).

Not long after the start one of my orderlies was killed while I was talking to them —by an accidental shell of our own.

Somewhere about 10 o'clock the Colonel of the supporting battalion and myself moved forward. The advantage of being with him was that it made communication with my widely-scattered guns easier. He was also an old friend from the days of Loos and earlier.

We went up to our front line, and on to and across the "racecourse." It is always a strange sensation when you find yourself walking in daylight over that strip of ground that would have meant instant death any time the past year or more.

It was pretty quiet our side of the " race-course," but biggish shells were falling on the other side. One dropped fairly adjacent, and I was glad to jump down into a German sap, with a tripod I had picked up, and some Lewis gun ammunition. The Colonel stayed to speak to one of his Captains he found wounded in a shell-hole, when another shell arrived which I was afraid had him. However, it didn't. Then I realized that two lines of Pioneers were steadily digging away at two communication trenches across the " racecourse " ; that they had been there for some time, and would be for many hours more. I think it was a magnificent bit of work —judging by my own feelings at that corner. They lost about 25 per cent, I believe, but made two fine trenches.

The Colonel established his H.Q. in a dug-out in the German front line. The Boche was by then putting a really heavy bombardment on to that line, luckily a little short. The trench seemed rocking, and the parados was going up in all directions. It rather reminded one of Portland Race !

I had nothing to do then but wait for

reports—it was too rough to go and look for the guns, and besides my place was to be where I could be found. All had gone well : the guns reached their objectives, luckily with small loss. The *nettoyeurs* (people who clear out the deep dug-outs — a most important job, as otherwise the Boche emerges and takes you in rear) had done their work well ; and in front the Redoubt was in our hands.

Before starting, by the way, I had watched the other Brigade going for the village, which lay on the top of a rise across a valley. They had little opposition getting into it, though they were badly shelled there afterwards.

The day was a hot one and the very deep dug-outs stuffy.

Reports came in, and I was able to tell Brigade H.Q. where the guns were—to their great relief. In the early afternoon I started to trek round, things being much quieter.

You have read accounts of how the entire ground comprising the German lines was ploughed up. They could not be exaggerated. The trenches were three parts obliterated : the whole surface was merely a

succession of shell-holes. There were a good
many Germans lying about, and some of
our own people ; but the cost of the advance
was not heavy, except to the left battalion,
caught by machine-gun fire from the left,
where the next Division had not got on.
Parties were wandering about, bringing up
stores and consolidating. The Boche shell
fire had become quite light.

I examined and readjusted gun positions,
and then went back to our own lines to see
about fetching up supplies, ammunition
belts, etc. The "racecourse" was quiet
then. I established a depot in the German
front line (I abandoned it afterwards when
I realized the other half of the dug-out had
already fallen in on the top of three or four
Germans) and then went and got some grub
with the Colonel. All my three officers were
all right, and two of them came back for a
meal to the depot. I slept on the staircase
of the battalion H.Q. dug-out —rather disturbed by constant " S.O.S." calls from the
people in the village, which was heavily
counter-attacked, unsuccessfully.

We were up at dawn —a very wonderful

dawn, the sun coming up among piles of golden cloud—and the village was again attacked. The Boche put a barrage of smoke shells between us and the village, but they were very ineffective. Soon things quieted down.

I went round to some of my positions and found them all serene. None of the guns had had a chance of firing. On the way back I found two of our infantrymen lying in a trench, both badly hit in the leg. They told me they had been there since 8 o'clock the morning before, and asked if I could help them. They were not complaining, but were quite cheery. I got stretcher bearers and came back. I said " I'm afraid you're rather badly hit." All they said was " How did it go ? " I was able to tell them we had done everything we were asked, and read them a very warm telegram from the Corps commander about the splendid fighting of the Division. " Then it's worth it," they said—and that was all, except to ask if the C.O. had got through. I thought it magnificent and moving beyond words.

The day passed quietly. The battalions were relieved in the afternoon, but not the guns. I saw the Colonel go away with regret, and then was called right back to Brigade H.Q. to discuss relief. They seemed very comfortable and snug, having their dinner in a good dug-out; the contrast with the scene I had just come from, and was going back to, was rather striking.

I was kept hanging about there till 3 a.m., and then got a few hours' sleep in our own rear position.

Next morning I was back in the German trenches early to see about the relief. We had had a German machine - gun handed over to us, which came in rather handily, as one of our own was damaged. This gun formed part of our armament for some days, though we did not have occasion to fire it. We found plenty of German ammunition. The trenches had been cleared a lot during the night, and were more recognizable.

I had to leave 4 guns in for another day, but got the rest out to our old dug-out behind our lines. There we had a bottle of champagne that I had had the foresight to

have sent up ! Somebody else had drawn
our rations ; and the Brigade hadn't told
us about our rum, so some one else got that
too ; and then the Brigade tried to curse
me for drawing rations twice. This was a
little too much ; but, as a matter of fact, I
found that the zest of a fight with the
Brigade was rather a good counter-irritant
to all the happenings of the last thirty-six
hours.

That night I sat on our parapet back
there, and watched the endless flashes, rockets
and shooting lights round —rather further out
than before, the latter were. We slept well.

We hung about next day till the afternoon,
and then were ordered right back. The men
marched out extremely cheery : I looked
behind me, and saw beaming faces wearing
(some of them) German helmets and playing
(one of them) a mouth organ.

The feeling in the air was very different
from what we felt coming out from the Loos
fighting. Then we had been hanging on for
a week by the skin of our teeth. This time
we really did feel that we were on top of the
Boche.

After two or three days out we went in to the attack again. The Brigade attempted to take a wood, and got one end of it —but at considerable cost. The French were attacking on our right, and at one period of the day I ran up against one of their *commandants*. He was a very nice fellow, and we concerted plans as to how my machine-guns were to cover his men. He spoke of probable losses ; but, said he, " l'infanterie c'est l'arme de sacrifice."

After this attack we were withdrawn to rest.

.　　.　　.　　.　　.

We are right back in a place behind Amiens, bathed in the deepest summer peace. No sounds of the guns reach us. Behind this farm, among its big trees, is a charming garden ; Madonna lilies and roses mix with onions and peas ; rosemary and potatoes, pinks and turnips, currants, strawberries, peonies all jostle each other. This afternoon all was basking in the sunshine, a fresh breeze stirred the trees, and there was a pleasant accompaniment of birds' songs and farmyard sounds. On one side of

the garden was an orchard, where some red
cows, ready for milking, were grazing eagerly
on the old pasture, across which long
shadows fell. Rich fields of corn and other
things lay round the farm, and in the near
valley, and between the woods on high
ground opposite, where a little church stood
up.

Far away across the Somme miles of unbroken fields sloped up to the horizon, with
here and there a dark clump of trees or a
wood that served to mark the distances.
Utter and most refreshing peace and beauty
brooded over the whole.

.   .   .   .   .

How do you like this for a bit of inter-
national language ? I heard one of our men
trying to explain to a French landlady that
the Boche had been nearly wiped out in the
fighting. His words were " Kamerad na
poo " !

LETTER 33

H.Q., M.G. Coy.,
27.7.16.

I will carry on the tale from my last. On leaving the quiet and familiar neighbourhood where we spent two or three days, we came up to our old fighting ground. On the third night we were in a little valley leading down towards our original front line.

It is rather thrilling to see the "racecourse" full of camps, the roads, silent so long, crowded and bustling, and even the railway that led straight from our lines to the Germans, reviving. I went over to see one of the villages just behind their lines. One could take a more detached, newspaper-correspondent sort of interest in it than when the line was still hot, so to speak, with fighting. Our artillery performance on it had been, as usual, wonderful, but the attack more wonderful still, for dug-outs and

157

machine-gun emplacements still survived. The latter are over-praised, I think—they are quite ordinary, as a rule, but the gun, if it survives, does the damage. In one there were piles of empty cases, and dozens of belts ready for use. That man had made a hobby of collecting British 18-pounder cases—he had quite a pile of them, neatly stacked, in his dug-out. There were many German bombs about, but the place had been pretty well cleared up. The village itself was more flattened than any I have seen before. Concrete had been lavishly used in dug-outs.

Their expenditure in material must be enormous. They line dug-outs and staircases with thick squared timbers where we only use a few props. Cavalrymen were prospecting in the village, cyclists were repairing the roads, motor lorries were going through one way, motor ambulances coming back the other.

We spent the next day happily in the valley, wondering at the roar of great guns and their activity. That night the Boche treated us to the best firework display I've

seen yet. For quite half an hour the sky
was lit by his Verey lights —never less than
10 up at a time—varied with a few coloured
ones. I believe there was an attack on.
Then I suppose his supplies gave out.

On the next day we moved up for opera-
tions. I walked over to our old part of the
world about 7 in the evening. They were
shelling some batteries, and, as before,
dropping a lot in the trench outside Brigade
H.Q. A summons there was not attractive.
Having seen the Brigadier, and the sections
attached to the leading battalions (4 guns
to a battalion), I repaired to the old German
front line, where was the last battalion—
my H.Q. were to be with it.

It was rather a cold and gloomy evening.
A nice little fire was going in the side of the
trench, however, and some hot tea was very
welcome. Somewhere about 11 I found
the head of the battalion, which was just
about to move up.

The bombardment going on at that moment by our guns was heavier than anything I have heard before, even on July 1st.
The reports made one continual roar, the

shells overhead a constant scream, and the flashes on the clouds never were still. The flashing effect reminded one of a bad cinematograph. Otherwise it was very dark. We started off in single file, threading our way over trenches and with difficulty avoiding our own guns, which roared hot flame at you from unexpected corners.

Our H.Q. were to be in the same Brickworks dug-outs that I was in last time. We got there at length and settled down for the night. Wonderful dug-outs they are too—a suite of them, twenty feet below the surface, entirely sheathed in wood, leading by staircases out of a long gallery eight feet deep.

Here, I believe, a German Colonel was caught the first day, shaving. When they told him the English were coming he said " Nonsense." They came, however.

The attack was to be on a village 1000 yards in front of our line. Two battalions were to carry it out, and I had a section with each.

Just before dawn there was a great thunder of guns, and with the first light they were off. We could not see what was happening, but soon could hear heavy rifle fire.

Then reports began to come back—at first rosy, as they always are ; then it began to be clear that the attack was not succeeding. The Boche kept up his usual barrages on the much-fought-through woods near the Brickworks, with occasional attentions to the Brickworks itself. The left battalion had been given an extremely difficult job— to start off diagonally and turn up to the left when it was opposite its objective. In the dark and smoke it turned too soon, and struck advanced trenches held by us. It did no harm there, but came no more into the story. The right battalion went straight at the village. It got across all right, but the wire was not cut, and it could not get in. It was 800 yards away across the open; and we heard nothing whatever more about it the whole day, and nothing at all about the four guns who were supporting it.

I got very anxious indeed about these. All the other guns I got reports from—they

M

did not suffer much—but not a word could come back from the fringe of the village. It was known that the attack had completely broken up ; and, to tell the truth, I did not much expect to see any but one or two wounded men of that section again. Darkness fell, and the remains of the battalion withdrew, with the rest of the Brigade. I sent back the other guns and waited, in case stragglers should bring in news. By midnight none had come, and I gave up hope. As I was setting off, with one or two signallers and oddments, a wounded sergeant came in who said he had seen the officer of the section hit, near the Boche wire, and that he thought he had got in, as his servant was with him ; but he knew nothing of the guns.

We walked back by way of a village, now in French occupation, that I had known well when our line ran through it. We trudged up in the dust, sticking to the road to avoid our own guns. Ambulances passed us, guns flashed on each side. We crossed the old " racecourse," and so up to the village, where the château wood was burning

—or rather a store in the wood. The village was full of French troops on the march, and (though we did not realize this at first) of gas. The Boche was putting over hundreds of small shells that whirred overhead and went off with a small explosion. We had noticed the old tear-shell smell, coming up the road; and that puts you off your guard. When we were nearly through the village I realized the smell was very queer, and we put on our gas helmets. But, as a matter of fact, it was not then thick enough to do anything but give one a bad taste in the mouth. As their shell gas does not take effect for eight or ten hours, I rather wondered what we should be like in the morning; however, we were all right.

The end of our journey was along the road on the ridge we knew so well. The Verey lights were going up—round the horizon, instead of just in front. An occasional great flare of red showed where the Boche had landed an incendiary shell—it bursts with a really enormous flame. We hit a forage cart coming to the valley where our present quarters are, and in that I peacefully slept. We got to camp and turned in.

You may imagine my delight on being woken up to hear that all four guns and teams were on their way back! And this was their story.

The officer and the guns started off from the wood after the last wave of infantry. It was dark, and when they got over to the other side the officer left the guns in shell holes 150 yards short of the village and went on with his servant (acting as orderly) to reconnoitre. He found that the assault had failed, and that there was no one between him and the German front trench.

He turned to come back, and was shot through the legs as he dropped into a shell-hole. His servant stuck to him, bound him up, spent the day with him in the shell-hole (50 yards from the Germans) and after dark crawled back to the section with him on his back. Then with another man he carried him into our lines, and landed him in an ambulance. A very fine piece of work, and he undoubtedly saved the officer's life.

Meanwhile the section had entrenched itself in three or four shell-holes, and mounted its guns. Its chance soon came; some Germans were spotted reinforcing over an open field. They opened on them with two guns—a little high. Some dropped, others made a dash for the German front trench. They had the range now, laid the guns on the middle of the field, and waited. Soon a big lot came along—60 or 70. They let them come on to their line of fire and then opened. Few of the Boches got away; they were almost enfiladed.

It is a surprising thing that the Germans took no measures whatever against these guns throughout the day, except a little unsuccessful sniping. The section got no more targets for the guns, but occupied themselves sniping Boches (they got several bombers, who were out after infantry in shell-holes) and boiling tea—for which purpose they had taken the precaution to bring candles. A couple of candles wrapped in a rag boil a canteen nicely, without making any smoke.

After dark they sent back for orders, though

they did not get to me. Finding the Brigade had moved, they retired with all their stuff at about 11 p.m. Since taking up the position they had not suffered a single casualty, except one man who would go from one shell-hole to another for a match.

It really was a very fine performance.

One man turned up a day later. He had been sleeping (apparently his strong point) when the section came in ; stayed in a shell-hole all next day ; came in after dark ; left his equipment in a shell-hole just in front of our line while he prospected ; crossed our front line unobserved ; found some people behind ; heard the news ; tried to get some sleep in a shell-hole there ; was shelled out ; went back across our front line to where his equipment was ; tried to go to sleep again ; was shelled out again ; nearly went back to the German line for his canteen and waterproof sheet which he'd left behind ; rather regretted he hadn't ; got into our front line ; found a dug-out ; tried to go to sleep in that, when some one found him, and, not unnaturally, kept him awake with questions and finally marched

him off as a spy ! However, he cleared himself, and arrived here complaining of nothing
but want of sleep. He is a Manx man.

I suspect we shall be out for a bit now.

LETTER 34

H.Q., M.G. Coy.,
31.7.16.

WE have had a quiet week in this valley,
close behind the line : and I think we shall
now move right back for a bit.

I told you of our attack on Sunday week.
Yesterday the two other Brigades of the
Division tried the same task, not, however,
successfully—except that I understand they
nipped an enemy attack in strength in the
bud. Now I should think we are certain
to have an appreciable time for refitting.

We were in reserve for yesterday's attack.
It was a very hot day ; we settled down
alongside an old British trench, and hoped
for the best.

It struck me what an amazing scene of
desolation the landscape was, under that
blazing sun. The ground sloped down and
up behind us to the road—chalk trenches,

and thistles and weeds, and the remains of a village, and what should have been the regular line of big poplars along the road showing gaps and riven stumps here and there. This was the least desolate part of the view, for there were copses with leaves on the trees.

On the left was a long unbroken horizon distant 800 yards to a mile, the ground, sloping up to it, all weeds, thistles and trenches, and more pitted than the ground behind. This sky-line led to a village captured the first day —not a vestige of building to be seen, but rows of bare poles of trees, without a leaf, and only a few naked branches. Straight in front was desert —absolute desert —bare brown earth churned and tumbled, where the German lines had been, as far as one could see, and away to the right indefinitely. Behind this the mound of the Brickworks and the two woods : thinned, shattered, blasted, leafless. Round these woods and to their right, the clouds of dust and smoke of the Boche barrage, at various points of the desert, puffs of dust where our guns were firing, ambulances working across

the desert, by a road there is there, which
has been made good. Otherwise no incident
on the glaring brown waste that seemed to
stretch away and away to the right. Behind
us, to the right was another village, where
a battered manor-house looked down an
avenue of leafless trees.

For orchestra, of course, the constant
guns.

In the whole broad view (and it was an
extensive one) there was not one square
yard that looked as it had been in peace,
that meant anything but destruction, or
that was anything but the broken shell of
an extinct civilization.

We stayed up there all day, and in the
evening were allowed to return here. Our
services had not been required.

LETTER 35

H.Q., M.G. Coy.,
9.8.16.

WE came out a week ago, and first of all
went back to some beautiful country beyond
Picquigny. We marched away from the
valley before dawn, so as to escape the heat ;
entrained 6 or 7 miles back, where German
prisoners were cleaning up the Station ; and
detrained in the afternoon, with a 10-mile
march before us. I took the company down
to a delicious meadow under some trees,
between a pool and a river. There they
bathed or washed, and made their little
fires, and were quite happy. It was still hot
when we marched off, but soon cooled down.
We went through beautiful wooded country
along a river. After 6 miles or so we came
to a village straggling up a steep hill. In
front of a house at the top of the hill was a
lady and her maids and man waiting with

buckets and jugs and carafes of cider. I couldn't believe at first that she meant to give a drink to all the men ; but she did, and we halted and lay down in the shade, while the party went round with tumblers, and every one got a most refreshing drink. We gave her three cheers and moved on.

We got in, later, to our destination—a beautiful small château, 18th century, surrounded by rare and specimen trees. There was a great tulip-tree behind the house, in the open by itself, with tall firs, Wellingtonias, beeches and other trees round. The Count was at the front, and did not live there, anyhow. There was a good deal of old-fashioned furniture and pictures about, and roses galore round the sweep in front, and the village church at the gate. The curé's sister was caretaker, but the curé was at the wars.

To our great disgust we had to march back again next day, to entrain for our old haunts up here. It was very hot marching back. I halted again in the village with the hill, and, once more the lady and her party came out and distributed cider all round. The men marched out of the village whistling the " Marseillaise."

I stole half an hour to give the men a dip from the same meadow, and then we entrained for here. It is all very familiar, though I didn't expect to see it again. Flat as it is, it looks very beautiful in the sunny weather, with all the crops ripe. But one has all the time a feeling that some grinning Horror is hiding behind this peaceful picture, and may poke its head through at any moment.

LETTER 36

I HAVE found these parts pleasanter than I expected. I remembered it last in November mud and rain. At present, with nice summer weather, and the crops and trees out, it is rather beautiful, in spite of the flat marshiness.

The town was rather badly shelled soon after we first arrived; on a market day too. I went in a day or two afterwards, and the townspeople were full of stories of how well the British troops had behaved, rescuing, stretcher bearing, and so on. Particularly there were stories of officers and men who had lost their lives trying to save children. One officer was found in a cellar with a child in his arms. They were trying to find two sappers who had gone back into a house where two children were.

I had a breezy morning up in the trenches

the other day. I was going round with my
friend the Colonel. First a "football" of
ours dropped short, and went off with a lot
of noise just the other side of the parados.
Then we went to look at a bit of trench the
Boche had knocked in, and when we were
well up it he proceeded to knock it in again.
I came out of that in double quick time, and
we lay up comfortably in a recess till the
air cleared. The Boche lifted on to the
support line and our guns got busy in reply,
both going very close over the top of the
parapet, so that one felt like the tennis net
during a hard rally.

Then we moved back and ran into it
again in a communication trench. While
we waited for that storm to blow over we
realized that under the grating on which
we stood were two men having their lunch.
They had been digging sump holes, and
retired into one of them, pulling the grating
over the top to keep off bits. It was quite
a Bairnsfather touch.

.   .   .   .   .

Last week, while on our way up, we met
two rather attractive small boys.

Maurice appeared first. We had come into a farm a couple of miles behind the line one hot evening. The farm—a large one—was not touched by shell, but it was empty and bare, and had been used as a billet for troops coming to and leaving the line for many months; so that it was not in the best repair. A family lived in the kitchen and an outbuilding.

We pitched our tent in the orchard, or rather among the withered skeletons of fruit trees; for horses had barked them all. After dinner we set the gramophone going. Soon a small person appeared in the twilight —half moonlight, half firelight—and knelt near the music-box, listening. He had a refined little face and a very gentle voice, and proceeded to make conversation for us.

They used to have a gramophone, he said, in the Cinema; but there they had a lady to play the piano as well. We asked where he came from. He said from La Bassée; that they had fled before the Germans and got down to Calais; that there they took ship for England, but were turned back when

within a kilometre of the English coast, and
sent on to Havre ; that they had stayed
there some time. " And there," said Maurice,
" was a gentleman who was very good to us
and gave me new clothes for my first Communion." Then, last year, his mother heard
the English were breaking through the
Germans and she would be able to get back
to their home. So they came up here.
" And here," said he, " we stay. My mother
works in the fields ; my father lives in
Béthune, and looks after horses, and we go
to school."

We were conscious of another and much
smaller figure, which had appeared alongside of Maurice. Its most noticeable feature
was an enormous briar pipe, from which it
puffed tobacco smoke with a good deal of
swagger. Just then there were loud and
determined cries from the house informing
Gaston that it was time to go to bed. He
shuffled uneasily for a bit ; but Fate came
nearer, and he departed reluctantly to
meet it.

Next day we saw rather a lot of Gaston.
He came and chatted with us before we

N

got up, and told us (quite untruly) that, though it was holiday time, they went to school for an hour every day. He asked for tobacco for his pipe ; for the authority that could send him to bed seemed quite unable to stop him smoking.

He looked like an imp, in very composite garments and boots much too big for him. At times the devil entered into him, and then he would prance round the horse lines, using the most regrettable English phrases with the most convincing accent, making believe to flog the horses, imitating the Sergeant-Major with considerable talent, throwing stones at Maurice (whose efforts at discipline were a miserable failure), completely self-possessed and as cheeky as a sparrow.

Stone-throwing, indeed, seemed to be a family habit ; for at one period of the morning there was a *mêlée*, in which a sister of 16, and her friends, joined. Their object appeared to be to kill each other with stones, bricks, or a large tent-mallet, picked up and hurled with their utmost force, but, luckily, with indifferent aim. In between

times Gaston trolled a catch of his own
composing, the refrain of which ran :

Bully beef,
Confiture.

with some more that we could not catch.

Revolver practice interested him extremely, and he begged for the empty brass
cases. " They are so useful," he said, " as
ink-pots." " Ink-pots ? " we queried. " Yes,"
he said. " You can hang one of them
by a string on your coat button and finish
your exercise as you go to school." " But
you cannot write walking along," we ob-
jected. " No, of course," said Gaston,
" You stop when you want to write."

There was nothing more to be said.

During the afternoon he became rather
impossible. The limelight was too much for
him. The pipe was more than ever in evidence, and he played shamelessly to the
gallery. Finally, he had to be led aside and
chastised, gently but firmly ; after which
he deserted our part of the orchard to go
and play football with the men. There at
last he was literally put out of counten-
ance by receiving the ball in his face.

Whereat Gaston (oh, what a falling off was there!) wept and was seen no more.

.   .   .   .   .

Late that evening I had gone to my blankets, but the transport officer, who shared the tent with me, and who had alternately chastised and encouraged Gaston, had not come back from the trenches, whither he was conducting rations.

I was reading in bed, when a small figure appeared in the doorway, shading a lighted candle with its hand. "Bon soir, m'sieu." No trace of swagger now ; a sweet, pleasant little voice. "Bon soir, Gaston." "Votre camerade n'est il pas rendu?" "Non; il reviendra peut-être à minuit." "Voulez vous lui dire bon soir pour moi?"

Gaston will break hearts yet.

LETTER 37

BATTALION HEADQUARTERS,
October, 1916.

ONCE more I am commanding a battalion.
A vacancy occurred in one of the old
regiments of the Brigade, and I was put in.
We have been through a lot of shows together, last year and this, so I am among
old friends.

We came down again to this part of the
world a few days ago, and, although we are
presumably here to be thrown in, I think
every one is glad to be away from the swamps
and heavy flat ground of the north, and
back on these hills, with their wide views
and fresh breezes.

We are well behind the line, training hard.

LETTER 38

YESTERDAY some of us went up to the
front, or near it, to reconnoitre. When I
say near it, we were half a mile ahead of
our successful push of July 1st, and 3 miles
behind the front line! Not a Boche shell
was to be heard or seen.

We went up in a bus—4 hours, over roads
mostly very rough and being mended by
Germans. We passed the church where
the great Madonna on the tower is leaning
downwards over the edge and offering the
Child to earth instead of to heaven.—Why
it doesn't fall is a marvel. I fancy the
weight of the base balances the figure.

We arrived (by bus) at the village captured by this Division on July 1st. There
is not a scrap of wall six feet high, the
German shelling after it was taken was

almost as bad as ours before. There again we met the Virgin. The church is absolutely flat, except for two small brick piers that used to support the altar, I should think. From somewhere (I should imagine from some vault or cellar) there has appeared one of the plaster statues of the Virgin you find in every church, a gracious enough figure in blue robe with head bent forwards and hands stretched out. This has been placed on the brick piers; and there, with its delicate lines, its attitude of sympathy, and its sweet colouring, presides over the mess of rubble that once was the church and village, and the riven poles that once were trees. It was pouring with rain when we arrived, and the mud and discomfort around added to the contrast.

We went a little way forward, but not far, as there was not time. The troops there are very confident and in great spirits. They feel they have the mastery over the Germans, and constantly move forward. We do not wire our trenches there now.

And there I saw some tanks. Wallowing in the slime as if it were their native element

—wriggling and twisting and creeping un-gainly away—they looked well, happy and in the best of form. They had a few scars from shells, but nothing to matter much. I walked alongside one as it shuffled along and talked to a man inside. He said it was great sport, that they hadn't yet met a trench they couldn't cross, that 100 men surrendered when his tank came along one day, and that they had dealt with wire and a village.

LETTER 39

IT is just a month since I brought the battalion out of the trenches in front of Bapaume. I will try and give a connected account of what was certainly the worst ten days I had in France, and what the battalion said was the worst they had had since they landed in Belgium in 1914.

After I last wrote we went to Montauban, where we waited our turn to go up, as a Brigade, and push. The other two Brigades of the Division went in the day before us. They were to push first.

The day before we moved up to the line was a little bit tense. It was a fine sunny day. Alongside our camp the never-ending stream of lorries ploughed its way through the mud of the Mametz-Montauban road.

We started through Montauban in the

185

first light, and made northwards. The front line was perhaps 3 miles away. There was only returning traffic on the road just then, and a big lorry was blocking it, stuck at a place where the bricks of the village, used to repair the road, were all churned up. Most of those villages have been spread over the roads.

We went on, past Trônes Wood and Longueval on our right, and came to a dump where we were to draw our bombs, tools, and sandbags, called Thistle Dump. The other battalions were before us, and we formed up on the grass with a couple of hours to wait. It was a chilly wind and not very cheery. We drew our stuff, and then moved on along a good communication trench (Greek Lane) to a supporting trench (Side Trench) on the right of High Wood, between it and Flers, about a mile and a half from the line.

There were no dug-outs in Side Trench and we began making " slits " for our H.Q. The place was not well chosen, however, being just in front of a battery ; and during the afternoon the Boche got several biggish shells in and about that bit of trench, so we moved to another one (Slope Trench) a little further on, also occupied by our battalion, containing the only dug-out in the neighbourhood. We shared it with a Company H.Q. The sharing, I'm afraid, was rather like that of the cuckoo in the nest, some of the company officers finding shelters up above. It wasn't a trench that was shelled, though.

So far the ground had been pretty well cleared up. There were not many dead lying about —only a few in shell-holes; but there was an enormous amount of equipment —rifles, bombs, ammunition and every sort of gear. Rifles were commonly being used as posts for telephone wires. The fighting there had taken place perhaps a month before. One could walk about over the open, but the whole was under observation from a ridge half right, $2\frac{1}{2}$ miles away.

The next day the other two Brigades attacked. They were to go over without artillery preparation at two o'clock in the afternoon. It was a beautiful afternoon, very clear and sunny. From Slope Trench

one looked over a very wide expanse of
country. On the right, Flers, and beyond
it Gueudecourt. Beyond again, Le Transloy
and Les Bœufs. Flers consisted of a few
wrecks of houses among some shattered
trees, ¾ of a mile away. The others were
little patches of wood and houses, more or
less on the horizon. A broad white gable
among trees marked Les Bœufs. In front
was the Bapaume ridge, perhaps 3 miles
off, with the two church steeples of the town
showing. Between us and Bapaume were
the villages of Ligny and Ligny Thilloy,
half-way up the ridge, hardly showing
among their trees. On the left front was
the Butte of Warlencourt—a large chalk
tumulus—with an old farm and a big wood
behind it. To the left again was Eaucourt
l'Abbaye—a house or two in a hollow—and
Lesars—a few battered houses on a ridge,
once wooded. Behind us were High Wood,
on our left rear, and Delville Wood on the
right rear.

Wherever trenches had been bombarded,
the ground was utterly churned up. The
rest of the view consisted of long slopes,

pitted of course with shell-holes, but greenish. One such slope led up to a small intermediate crest between us and Bapaume ; and our front line was just the other side of this. The villages behind the Boche line were not much damaged. Here and there a hedgerow of willows or a sunken road made a detail.

At a quarter to two we were standing in a bay in Slope Trench, watching this wide and peaceful view. An occasional shell was being sent over from our side—just the normal luncheon time dropping fire ; otherwise all was quite quiet. Even these seemed to fall off towards the hour.

Then it crashed out. First one battery started rapid fire ; and at once it was taken up, right and left, all along our front. It was a tremendous noise—crack, crash, bang, scream, in all directions. The flashes of the guns could be spotted for miles. At the same time contact aeroplanes began cruising about over the line, quite low.

We could see our supporting troops advancing in long lines up the slope in front ; and the Boche barrage fire was soon dropping among them—not apparently doing much damage, but throwing up great black fountains. One of our aeroplanes was hit, and fell, crumpled. It lay on the slope in front, not far from a tank, deserted some weeks before.

Gradually the firing subsided. We heard later that the attack had been a complete failure, being caught by machine-gun fire. Two of our old battalions had gone over the parapet and suffered severely. That night our stretcher bearers were called for to help in the long two-mile carry that was necessary before the wounded could be got to the ambulance.

Next day we moved up. It had been rather difficult to keep the petrol tins filled with water (each company carried a certain number as a water reserve). We were told we could draw from Flers; but Flers was always being shelled, and, besides, the wells were under the ruins. Our intelligence officer got hit looking for them. We could draw some, but not much, from High Wood, that being in the area of another Division.

We moved up in the afternoon, H.Q. going last. The route was first of all by Greek Lane, then along a bit of road in a little valley, then along a deep narrow trench by Abbey Road, and then up an extremely unpleasant trench known as Swan Alley.

The bit of open road was rather a favourite shelling ground. I followed the last company with signallers and staff; and we turned into the road and began going along it in small parties.

It was getting towards dusk, and the Boche chose that moment to get " wind up." I was two-thirds the way along the road when they began to plump heavy stuff very close to it, and behind. We most of us reached the trench —a deep one, under the shelter of the rise; one or two of the men behind were blown to bits.

Then for about 20 minutes the air was absolutely thick with shells. Our Brigade had called for retaliation : and there was constant whir and scream overhead. We were quite snug in our trench, however. It really is very snug when you are quite safe, with shells dropping over.

The storm died down, and we moved on. Our destination was two support trenches, just dug, leading off Swan Alley, 800 yards behind the front line. The companies had already arrived there, and the battalion we were relieving had departed. Its C.O. was waiting for me. I asked where his H.Q. were, and he pointed to the surrounding bit of Swan Alley and cleared out.

Swan Alley, as I said, was really very unpleasant. It had once been a Boche communication trench. It had been taken by us a week or two before, and many of its former garrison were left, half sticking out of the floor and sides of the trench. There were a good many of the attackers too—mostly along the parapets. The smell in parts was sickening. There were, of course, no dug-outs—just one or two little holes scooped out of the side of the trench.

The men were in the two new trenches I spoke of. These were so narrow that one could not pass along them. I set them on to improving them, and turned to making a home for myself.

It was dark now. I selected one of the

recesses to sleep in, and hung my water-proof sheet over the opening. I didn't quite like the air inside, though. There was a nasty softish bump in the floor of the trench outside that I suspected—with reason, as I saw next day. The Lewis gun officer, making a hole for his thigh in the recess next door, soon stopped that.

I lay down for a few minutes ; and then they began to shell. They had two guns somewhere on the right that caught the two new trenches in enfilade. They were a little wide at first, and going well over Swan Alley ; then they got the line better. Soon I heard that a shell had dropped almost in one of the trenches.

Not much damage yet, however. I went out to see how they were getting on with the work. I got half-way along the second trench, as far as to the right of " A " Coy., and found out what they were doing. I thought of going on to the end, as they told me the officers were there ; but then thought I wouldn't, as it wasn't too healthy on top, and went back to my hole. Shortly afterwards the Sergeant-Major came to tell me

o

that a shell had dropped into the trench where the officers of " A " Coy. were having a meal, and had knocked out four of them. Two were killed, and one died soon afterwards. The other was very badly hit.

About then the Boche shortened a little, and shells began to fall round Swan Alley. When a dud landed with a thud just behind my hole I thought it time to move, and settled down again 100 yards further down the trench. Here I got some sleep, on a couple of ammunition boxes, alongside the Doctor, and was conscious of the shelling throughout the night at intervals of about $\frac{3}{4}$ of an hour. Our losses by the morning were 20 men and 5 officers—a bad start. The Brigadier came along at dawn and cursed us for blocking the communication trench.

Next morning we relieved a battalion in the front line. Swan Alley got worse and more knocked about as it got forward. The relief went without incident ; the Colonel showed me the Boche dug-out he used as H.Q. and the new trench the Boche had dug about 80 yards away, and I settled in.

The state of affairs was very mixed up there. We held Bind Trench and Bind Support up to a point, after which the Boche held both. This point was a communication trench, the continuation of Swan Alley, known as Snap Trench. On the right of this the Boche front line consisted of a trench called Rifle Trench. Our battalion left was a little to the left of Snap Trench, and after that the line became very involved, the next battalion coming almost in front of us. We held three bombing blocks (on Bind and Bind Support and Snap Trenches) and our right was in Bind Support, a narrow and dilapidated trench, close to the Boche in parts. There was no wire in front of us anywhere.

The H.Q. dug-out was a good one, six or eight feet below the surface, down a few steep steps. Outside the opening (which of course faced the Boche) was a strong cover over the trench of heavy beams.

We remained in without much incident for 24 hours, and then were relieved. We went back to Flers Trench, near Brigade H.Q., ¾ of a mile back.

We made our H.Q. in an old gun-pit. This had its disadvantages, as the Boche occasionally strafed them, or at least the existing battery position not far off. However, it was pretty comfortable. We used to leave it when they started and come back when they had done. They never fell particularly near. On one of these rather hurried excursions I tumbled into some wire and tore my clothes (it was pitch dark), ran into our own battery, and then got completely lost. I really hadn't the vaguest idea of the direction of anything, and contemplated a night out. However, by shouting I got back to Flers Trench and so home. That night we sent up a company to cut a new trench (New Cut) across a re-entrant in the front line.

Next day the rain began—a steady drizzle. We were to go up again in the early afternoon. One of the trenches the men were occupying got badly shelled before we started. I led the battalion up by Greek Lane—the main communication trench we were told to use. The way got longer and longer, and we didn't come to anything I recognized ; yet there were the name boards along the trench, beautifully clear, " Greek Lane." At last I knew we must be wrong, as we were about to top a rise and come in view of the Boche ; there was nothing for it but to turn the battalion about in the trench and go back again. It subsequently turned out that there were *two* main *divergent* communication trenches, both called Greek Lane ! This labelling is so useful.

The turning about had got the battalion wrong end first, which rather delayed the relief ; however, it was completed at last, and once more we settled into the front line.

We knew, of course, that we were there for an attack ; and I was called back the next day to Brigade H.Q., which were in very good dug-outs back by the sunken road. There I met the other C.O.'s, and the Brigadier expounded the scheme to us.

I did not very much care for the scheme. It was to be an attack just before dawn, and we were to be the right of it. Nothing was to happen on our right, and there was to be a gap on our left round the complicated

network about Snap Trench. Beyond that
one battalion was to do a very difficult
attack across diagonal trenches ; beyond
them another was to go over. The Division
on the left was doing something. The
German trench opposite me, to the right of
Snap Trench, was, you will remember,
Rifle Trench, and I was told to :

1. Go across and take 400 yards of Rifle
Trench frontally

2. Make a defensive flank back to our
front line on the right

3. Make a bombing attack up Bite Trench.

I insisted on this : it was obviously necessary to do something in the middle ; and
for all this I had by now less than 500 men.
By the time we started I had not 450 and
only about 14 officers all told. The frontal
attack was thus going to be extremely thin,
while the defensive flank as marked at H.Q.
by a few blue dashes with a chalk pencil
was about 500 yards long.

I returned to the front line. When we
first got there the previous day, by the way,
a man had been brought before me suffering
from shell-fright. He was a miserable sight

—a smallish youth, lately a grocer's assistant, with the eyes of a frightened hare, and his mind obsessed with terror. He looked this way and that as I spoke to him, could not answer coherently and was a thorough wrec k I tried to get him on to the price of sugar, to turn his mind on to familiar things, but it was no good, and I sent him down.

We passed two or three days waiting in the trenches. Twice we withdrew almost every one while they gave Snap Trench a special bombardment. On these occasions I went back to the bottom of Swan Alley where the Doctor had rather a good dugout. A little beyond this was a specially, gruesome bit of trench, where a Boche hung head downwards over the parapet into the trench. I wished his head would drop off and have done with it.

The date of attack was fixed at last. On the morning before I was going round our right, making preparations, with the bombing officer, when rather a curious thing happened—a thing that emphasized the unsettled state of affairs.

We were looking over the parapet to the

right of New Cut (the trench our company
had dug). The German line was 4 or 5
hundred yards away, where the ground
began to rise towards Thilloy, and there
was a sunken road opposite us. Suddenly
we spotted a figure in a grey greatcoat
coming towards us down the opposite slope.
He had just emerged from a fold in the
ground and was, I think, in front of their
line. He came steadily on. The bomber
suggested shooting, but I thought he must
be coming to surrender and should not be
put off. On he came till he was perhaps
350 yards away ; then he suddenly realized
his mistake and doubled back. Off darted
the bomber for a rifle (there were hardly any
men where we were—the line was absurdly
thinly held). He got one and began shooting,
but some way from me, so that I could not
tell him where his shots were going. Meanwhile the Boche was getting near the sunken
road. The bomber had a couple of shots,
both very short ; and then the Boche
dropped into the, road and out of sight.
Shortly after that we met the Brigadier
going round. I told him I thought my

front for attack was too big, and got 100
yards knocked off it. In the end our attack
started on a front of about 270 yards.

For days I had been reporting that our
right and centre were being worried by our
own big shells dropping into or very close to
our trenches. On this day in particular
there was a gun that steadily bombarded
the trench from behind with inexorable per-
sistence and deadly accuracy. The officer
commanding the right company kept on
reporting it, and I kept on telephoning to
Brigade about it ; but it was never owned
to by anyone, and never stopped.

. That afternoon preparations were complete. Three companies, about 270 strong
in all, were to do the frontal attack. Seven
officers remained for these three companies.
They were to start from a taped line that I
had had put out the night before, parallel
to Rifle Trench, about 300 yards from it,
in front of New Cut. They were to go in
two lines, with men about 2 yards apart,
and only a few yards between the lines.
One Vickers gun, from ·my old company,
went with them, and they took their Lewis

guns. They were to try and join up with the bombing attack up Snap Trench, on the left.

Two platoons of the fourth company were to go out on their right, one two-thirds of the way across, and one one-third, and dig in as a defensive flank. The remaining two platoons were to come across to the left, and support the battalion bombers, who were to attack up Snap Trench. Two companies of another regiment were to file into the trenches after midnight, when our people would have left them.

At the last moment a further objective was given us; but as we did not get the first, it made no difference.

There was to be no preliminary bombardment, but the guns were to open on Rifle Trench at 2.45, and lift after 3 minutes, when it was hoped we should be across. They were then to barrage behind.

· My H.Q. were to be in the dug-out in Bind Trench, moving forward to Rifle Trench as soon as that was taken.

We had withdrawn that afternoon for another bombardment of Snap Trench;

and we returned to the front liné somewhere about 5 o'clock. I got out my orders while we were back (it was then that final Brigade orders reached us) and talked over them with the two company commanders there. The right companies had not withdrawn, and I sent for their commanders after our return. I also kept one of the others at H.Q. for a bit, as I thought he wanted a rest before going over. They had had a very trying week already.

The dug-out was perhaps 10 feet square in addition to the steps, and had a recess in one side as well. A German shovel and gas helmet were hanging up. It was lined with wood, and a plank with a couple of boxes along one side served as a table. About five people could sleep on the floor.

The Brigadier came round and began to strafe about the company commanders not being with their companies; however, I told him I had sent for them. I let them rest for two or three hours. Then they went back to complete their preparations.

I had something to eat, and about 9 went out myself.

Steady rain had settled in for some hours, and the trenches were in a bad state. They were dug in clay, and were slimy and water-logged. I went along to the right of the line, to check the tape and the company fronts. The piece of Bind Support between Snap Trench and New Cut had been shelled out of recognition many times : and bits of it were mere tracks over mounds of clay. It was mostly too narrow for two men with equipment on to pass.

I scrambled and slid along this, and was soon covered in clay wash and slime. I tried to be cheery with the men as I passed ; but it was perfectly obvious they were out of heart, after their long exposure to shelling and with the atrocious weather conditions. Their rifles were nearly all unworkable with clay, and they knew it ; and that took the heart out of them too.

I got to New Cut, and found the end of the tape. I had no orderly with me, as all our orderlies and signallers had been used up. I set out along the tape, checking its direction by compass and pacing it out.

It was very lonely out there. There was

a fair amount of light —enough at least to
see a post against the sky. Occasional
German shells and bullets came over—not
specially close. The ground was pitted
with shell-holes ; and towards the far side
there were many of our dead lying, killed
in the attack a few days before. The tape
was twisted round rifles, stuck into the
ground by their muzzles.

I tracked it along, and at the end found
a company commander already getting his
men out. They were being hauled out of
Bind Support one by one (the trench was
deep and the parapet slippery) and made to
lie down in a row, along the line of the tape.
I was sorry he had begun so early ; it was
very damping out there on the wet earth
in the rain ; and, besides, those other figures
lying there, not on the line of the tape and
in varying attitudes, made rather ghastly
company.

I went back again, going backwards and
forwards between New Cut and the tape —
they were nearly 100 yards apart at the
end. That was the loneliest part —away
from all landmarks, with nothing but the

wind and the rain, and the crack or whiz
of bullet or shell, and the shell-holes and the
dead. One got a sort of unreasoning feeling
sometimes of clutching fear that one had
walked over the tape and was lost—fear
for the incomplete preparation, and fear
that one might drop wounded into a shell-
hole and be seen no more.

I got the company fronts marked out (they
proved quite satisfactory) and then met the
centre company making its way along New
Cut, where it was to remain till it got out
upon the tape. I placed them in position,
and then went to see after the left company.
There was rather more trouble here. A
platoon was missing; and the company
commander (a very good officer) had only
just come to France, and so was making
rather heavy weather of things—quite naturally, as it was all completely new and very
trying. But it was rather striking, and
made one realize the completely matter-of-
course way in which the others took these
tremendous things. I showed him his position, and went to look for his missing
platoon. I was having a word, of course,

with the men as I passed. One said, " The
truth is we aren't hardly fit for it, sir."
Well, it was the truth. Another said,
" We'll do our best for you."

I soon found the missing platoon. They
were blocked in the narrowest part of Gird
Support by the two platoons from the right,
who were to assist in the bomb attack.
The only thing to do was to get the latter
out of the trench, to lie down behind the
parados ; so I got on top and made them
follow, with some difficulty at first. I got
the platoon past, and saw it rejoin its company ; and then my work was done. I was
satisfied that all would be in place for the
start, and that the places were right. I
returned to my H.Q.

I had been unable, by the way, to move
the two platoons from right to left earlier
in the day, as the right was so *very* weakly
held.

I got back to the dug-out, and first took
off the jersey I was wearing, as the sleeves
had come down over my wrists and were
simply solid with clay. ' I borrowed a com-
forter that wasn't being used, to replace the

jersey. I then went out with the bombing officer, to see that his preparations were complete. Previously we had interviewed the bombing officer of the next battalion in the dug-out; they were to attack along Bind Trench and Bind Support to the left; but seemed rather casual about what is really a very delicate and complicated operation. As a matter of fact they never got beyond their blocks.

All was well except that the supporting company was filing in, and threatened to confuse matters. I got the place clear, but rather think some more came along afterwards and did check our own supports.

Back again to the dug-out, this time to sit down and await events. A watch hung on a nail in the wall above the candle on the table, and showed 20 minutes to go.

There were there besides myself the adjutant, the Lewis gun officer, and the signalling officer—all three aged from 19 to 22. The bombing officer, the last time he was in, had borrowed a revolver, and it was well he did so.

The minutes went by. Then at last there

was a crash and a roar, and the bombardment had broken out. Soon I went up to see what I could see. I walked a little way along the trench and looked over the parapet towards Rifle Trench. It had become impossible down below, picturing those two long lines moving across the dark and pitted no man's land, and faring one did not know how.

I looked across towards Rifle Trench. It was hell out there—shrapnel bursting, bombs exploding, our own barrage further on—it was one long crash and roar. And the Verey lights were going up in large numbers from Rifle Trench; and then I clearly saw, silhouetted against the Verey lights, some little black figures running —back. The attack had failed.

The combination of failure with the plight of the men out in that dreadful zone was almost too much; for their sufferings were vain. I went back to the dug-out. Presently the Brigade H.Q. rang up to ask for news, and I told them what I believed had happened.

Not long after this a figure dropped into

P

the dug-out, panting and excited. It was the bombing officer. I remember his face was a very light brown from being covered with clay that had dried, and that his lips and tongue and the rims of his eyes showed bright pink beside the clay, and his eyeballs very white. He told me that he and his bombers had taken the German block by running along the top of the parapet and parados and bombing from above ; that they had jumped down into the trench, and working along it found themselves blocked by a wire obstacle, probably kept ready to be let down into the trench for this purpose ; that before they had reached the obstacle they had started a heavy bomb fight with a German trench parallel to Snap Trench ; that he had returned to get up the supports, who were delayed ; that when he got back to the obstacle the two men he had left there were not there (in fact they had been hit) ; that, thinking they had got on, he got up on to the parapet and passed the obstacle that way, under heavy fire ; that he jumped down and then came to the mouth of this parallel trench ; turned into it ; met a German round the corner ; shot him with his revolver ; realized his men were not there ; came back, up and past the obstacle again ; found his men a good deal reduced and bombing hard ; decided it was impossible to get on while the parallel trench was held ; realized that the right attack had broken down ; decided to return to our old block, as it was better sited than the Boche block ; withdrew—and here he was to tell me.

It was some time before I got any direct news from the right. What had happened, however, was that the lines had gone across —somewhat raggedly perhaps, owing to the ground and the conditions—that they, or a great part of them, arrived within 30 yards of the Boche trench and collected in shell-holes, finding the trench full of Germans, who were keeping up a barrage of bombs ; that out of 7 officers who started with the three companies 5 were by that time hit ; that while the left began to waver under machine-gun fire and rifle fire, the right was thinking of charging in—when the left broke and went back and the rest followed.

There were between 100 and 150 casualties among the men.

I think the attack was too light to have much chance against a full trench. The other elements of failure were the weather conditions and the worn-out state of the men.

The two platoons on the right went out and dug themselves in all right ; and then had to come back.

I sent the adjutant along to find out how many men had got back and where they were; he found the officers organizing against a counter-attack, in case the Boche made one, as they rather expected he would.

Meanwhile it had got light ; and a message came from Brigade to say a tank was coming up, and on its arrival the attack was to be renewed. The tank was to come up on the left of the next battalion ; and I pointed out that this could not affect my right, that if the men could be got out of the trenches again it would only be to be mopped up by machine-gun fire, and that I had under my immediate command the remains of two bombing sections and a strange company from another regiment. So they compromised for a renewal of the bomb attack. The bombing officer, himself as brave as a lion, knew this would not now succeed, and was very much against it. However, I told him to make a bit of demonstration. It was really out of the question now to extemporize a first - class bombing attack out of our broken bits and a strange company.

Presently it was rumoured that the tank was around. We had been ordered to report its arrival at once. Now the code name of Brigade H.Q. was " EEL " and ours was " TROUT." A telegram was accordingly despatched in a few minutes which read " EEL. Tank approaching. TROUT."

In spite of all the gloom of failure and loss, nothing could make that tank anything but comic. We stood along the trench to watch it. First a humming sound, then the squat longish animal lurching along the Boche front line, every now and then firing a six-pounder gun that stuck out from the side ; no doubt firing its maxims too. On it came, nosing along the trench ; then, as if struck by a new idea, it turned off and went across to the Boche support line ; and then went away, nosing along that. It produced for a time quite an air of cheeriness in our part of the world. Boches were reported clearing out in the distance, and one of the Vickers guns opened on them —not with much effect, I think. The tank had a couple of men hit by armour-piercing bullets.

The Brigade wanted to know how our bomb attack had got on ; but it hadn't got on at all. The tank had not been near it, such as it was. Anyhow the parallel trench was still full of Germans, and I said so. They then said that a second tank was on its way and would deal with that trench, and we must then advance. I knew, and the bombing officer knew, that the men were totally unfit to attack at all ; however, on those definite orders we proceeded to organize a new bomb attack, backed by the totally strange company. But thank goodness the second tank stuck and remained behind our lines all the afternoon, drawing fire, but untouched. Eventually it got back all right.

The day wore on, and in the early after-

noon I was sitting on the floor of the dug-
out. Further in were the bombing and
signalling officers; on the steps was the
Lewis gun officer; the adjutant was standing at the entrance talking to some one,
and near him were the machine-gun officer
and the trench mortar officer. Suddenly
there was a very tremendous and imminent
noise, quite unlike anything else I have
experienced; and something had happened.
One knew at once of course that it was the
burst of a shell. For the moment all was
darkness and the earth dropping somewhere.
The first thing one did was to take stock of
oneself—no, unhurt. Then to look up and
see if we were buried. No—through the
cloud of smoke that filled the opening a
small light hole was visible.

Some one outside enlarged the hole, and
out we came. The Lewis gun officer, sitting
on the stairs, had been hit in the neck; he
went straight off, and we saw him no more.
The signaller, poor boy, was badly shell-
shocked. It came on worse after the first
half-hour, and he was practically unable to
speak or move till next day. The bomber,

with this on top of the fight, was pretty badly shaken for the moment. It was obvious he could no longer lead an attack. When I crawled through the opening, helped by the people outside, I saw that the shell had broken in the headcover, driving down the heavy beams, and had wrecked the opening of the dug-out. I stepped over two men lying just outside and climbed through the debris to the right, finding there the trench mortar officer lying dead. Coming back I found they were working to get out the adjutant and machine gunner—both just alive, lying among earth and beams. As they pulled the adjutant clear he gave a little quiver, and died.

The gunner was very badly injured in the legs—I think by falling beams. He was alive, and was carried down the trench to the dressing station ; but died soon after.

The mess corporal had a wonderful escape. He usually sat on the top of the stairs, using a shelf there as his pantry ; but he had just left it.

I felt that I must make it quite clear to the General that any renewal of the attack now by us was absolutely out of the question; so I went down to Brigade H.Q. I explained matters, and the General was quite sensible and nice. I also asked for some reinforcements, as I was holding something like ¾ of a mile of front with something like 300 shaken men, and the people on my right were vague and shadowy in the extreme. I got some of it taken off my hands next day.

While I was down there the General told me there was a job for me in England. I felt extremely pleased.

I slept heavily that night. I had sent for the last two available officers as reinforcements, and one of them took over Adjutant. We got people out looking for wounded; and I think the ground was pretty well searched. The bomber had recovered by now, and himself went to look for a wounded officer; but could not find him.

I went round to New Cut in the early hours to see how they were getting on. The same old game had begun; our own shells were landing with regularity and precision just in front and behind. Dawn came on, the stretcher bearers came in, and I went back.

That afternoon we were relieved. It had come on to rain again, hard. There was no question of troops passing in the narrow parts of Bind Trench, so I decided to withdraw my people before the others went in. The Boche did not seem at all like attacking ; every night and every morning he got " wind up " at nothing, and sent up red flares for artillery support, and plumped hundreds of shells behind us.

The withdrawal, however, was a little more complete than I had intended. The relieving battalion did not arrive at once ; and, going down Swan Alley (which was in an awful state of mud) to find them, I found a block caused by some oddments who were forcing their way in the wrong direction. I made a passage through, pushing men out of the way down dug-outs and on to fire-steps; and at last the stream flowed in the right direction. I was unpleasantly conscious that there was nothing whatever on our half-mile of front except one Maxim gun ; and I pushed the first people that arrived (a Lewis gun team) straight through, more as a patrol than anything else, to see that there were no Germans there! However, all was well, and the relief was quickly completed.

So at last we got back. Even then I had to leave two unfortunate subalterns to do duty for two days more in the front line, as the relieving battalion was so short. Counting them, and after having had up all reinforcements from the transport, I had 9 officers left besides myself.

The Doctor and I walked back together. We came over the top along Abbey Road, as there was no strafing going on. The ground up there had hardly been cleared at all. One chap in two halves was rather a gruesome sight.

There was confusion as to where we were to go that night, the Brigadier having told us Side Trench, the orders saying Flers Trench. I went to Flers Trench. There was six inches of water or mud in most of it. The men were so done that they lay in the mud and slept. We had a little dugout—a large recess really—and the Doctor

and I tried to keep warm there. It was no
use, however : our clothing was sopping
wet, and the temperature below freezing in
the open. We gave it up and got out to
walk on top (we were far behind the lines).
It was a clear, cold, starlit night, with a cold,
piercing breeze. One was chilled to the
marrow. I remembered that Brigade H.Q.
were not far off, and thought that one might
do better talking to the officer on duty. We
found our way across, after one or two
attempts, and descended into the warm
(comparatively) and lamp-lit corridor. The
Doctor would not wait, but I spent the night
there, and even got a little sleep in an un-
occupied corner of a bunk, curled round an
upright.

Next day the Doctor told them he would
not answer for the consequences if we
stayed where we were ; and got a sort of
half permission to move up to Side Trench
or Slope Trench, where some of our people
already were. We didn't wait to confirm
this (or get it withdrawn) but scuttled back
as quickly as we could. We got into Slope
Trench, where the good dug-out was (the

whole battalion could get into one trench now). There were strafings about it; but it would have taken something more like H.E. to get us out again, and we managed to stick to it all right.

There was frost again that night; and next morning I went round at dawn talking to the men. They mostly had their little fires going, and many of them had made quite snug little shelters and kept moderately warm. They were very nice and friendly, and offered me tea; and my standing jest, which came off with every group, was to tell them we were going out that afternoon, but that if any man wanted to go in the other direction I might be able to arrange it. A mild joke, but a great success. During the afternoon we got shelled again by long-range whizz-bangs—new to me. Another officer was hit. These big whizz-bangs give no warning of their approach, but suddenly go off above you with a great metallic clang. The subaltern was hit, not very badly, in the back. He was helped down into the deep dug-out, where there was a charcoal brazier burning.

He was very uncomfortable, turning over and trying different positions. At last the Doctor decided to give him morphine. " Are you going to send me off ? " he asked ; and when the Doctor said yes, " Cheero, you chaps," he said, looking round and waving his hand. He was one of the four who came back from the attack on Rifle Trench.

That evening we did go out. I walked back with the Doctor, took a moderately successful short cut outside Montauban, steering by the stars, and at length found myself once more at Pommiers Redoubt, with my successor there, waiting to have the battalion handed over to him. (He was a senior officer of the regiment, sent out from England for the purpose.)

I drew up my reports, said good-bye to every one, lunched once more with my old M.G. Company, interviewed the Divisional General when he came over (he wanted my account of things and said a few kind words) and then pushed off for Amiens and HOME.

LETTER 40

ENGLAND,
February, 1917.

I DON'T think I shall stay on at this job much longer. Soldiering at home, delightful as it sounds, has an atmosphere altogether its own; and one greatly misses both the cordial friendliness all round and the general knowledge of what really happens in a fight which are so characteristic in France, and so markedly absent in many places here.

LETTER 41

Corps H.Q.,
April, 1917.

I HAVE had a very pleasant month at these Headquarters. At first one felt rather the " new boy," as there was hardly anyone I knew here. That soon wears off.

This is a part of the line I have never seen before. It is not very far from the place I first went to in 1914 — the big observation hill that is on our right now could just be seen from my first billet. The other day I made a special effort to see the city.* I was on my way to the line, and started early, driving in a motor, with my servant as orderly.

The city is quite the most impressive thing I have seen in that way. You go in past the big asylum (much knocked about) into the outskirts (the boulevards there of

* Ypres.

better-class houses mostly have their walls
standing and parts of the roof on) to the
centre of the city. Some of this is mere
mounds of brick rubble : though a house
or two, notably the *mairie* at the end of the
square, have curiously escaped. This *mairie*
is an unpretentious white building ; it was
being repaired or painted, and the scaffold-
ing is still there. Whole streets remind one
of Pompeii with an extra story : and then
there is the great Hall and the Cathedral.

When I first went there the Cathedral had
a great bulwark of beautiful tower still
standing. It rose grandly, with graceful
Gothic panelling of stone, and ended in a
spike of masonry. It was a very dignified
and impressive sight—broken itself, yet
dominating the wasted town. The second
time I went up there it was gone : it had
itself slid to ruin. I was very surprised to
find how much I missed and regretted it.

But the saddest and grandest sight is the
great Hall. This was a long 16th century
building of brick (as all the big buildings
here are) stone faced, with a tower in the
middle, and slender graceful pinnacles at

Q

the ends. Of the latter one strangely remains absolutely untouched, every crocket perfect, the ornament on top unbroken. It seems to stand there in protest to the desolation round, a suggestion of what it all has been.

A good deal of the central tower is left, with its Gothic windows and panellings; but of the buildings only perhaps half the outer walls are left, and those much broken about. They were crowded with stonè detail, hundreds of statues nearly life-size between the windows, thousands almost of carved corbels and brackets. Those statues that remain are hacked and disfigured by shrapnel and bits of shell, and so is the stone arcading on the wall with its little shafts and arches, and the window tracery that shows against the sky. It is not a place to linger by, for the square is a favourite mark of the Boche: indeed, he can see directly into it on one side from his ridge.

We left the motor and walked through the square, as I had never had a good look at the Hall. Then we made our way past the Infantry Barracks and an old church

(the great bell has fallen and sticks out of
the tower half-way down) to some deep
recesses in the Ramparts that are said to
have been Marlborough's stables. Here I
breakfasted in a comfortable room with a
glowing log fire in an enormous open fireplace. Above the fireplace was a great
mantel-board with a carved edge supported
on two well-carved gilt heads. I don't
know whether it is on its original site or
not.

Then, after a talk with the commander
of a Machine-Gun Company whose guns were
in this part of the line, the orderly and I set
out by a road that would lead to an important town if one went through the Boche
lines. There are some nice old houses along
this road before one leaves the city—one in
particular, dated 17th century, with cheerful
stone cherubs and wreaths of flowers as
ornament. The roof is gone and the walls
are going, so their gaiety looks rather
crooked and crumbling, poor things.

We went out through the gate named after
the said town, where the road goes through
the Ramparts. These really have come into

their own. No shelling affects them much : they stand, first cousins to all the old city walls one has ever seen ; only instead of being out-of-date antiquities they are of the greatest value. We crossed a causeway over the moat, which here forms a broad lake, and so out along the road. At the entrances to the city the shell-holes are almost continuous.

The country between the city and the Boche ridges is flat wet land, dotted with châteaux and farms and a village or two, all of course smashed. The sky-line is nearly always Boche ; you get a feeling that they very much sit over us. As you get nearer the front line where we hold the edge of the high ground you get cover ; but in some places we don't hold the higher ground at all. In others there is a valley between us. Then, again, the circular shape of the line makes every side a front.

We walked out half a mile over the flat to another Machine-Gun Headquarters. There I picked up the officer commanding, called on the Brigadier, and set out for the line.

We worked up the slopes, partly by trench and partly not, and I tried to get the hang of the ridges and spurs and distant woods. The country looks curiously park-like. All the fields, of course, are fallows and covered with brown bent, and the slopes and the biggish trees round the châteaux give quite an impression of continuous park land. The last lap consisted of " duckboard " walk in the open under cover of the forward crest. This, however, is rather a favourite shelling spot, and the Boche had an observation balloon up. As we came along a couple of clangs in the air indicated that the Boche was having a shot at a carrying party ahead, which scattered promptly. I don't mind saying I ran over that bit. The boy behind me was too proud to.

We were now on the front-line system, which was on the slopes of a famous hill. I can't of course describe it in detail, but it included an extraordinarily interesting series of tunnels, lit by electric light. Every now and then one went up a staircase to the open air and peered cautiously over a breastwork at the desolation of churned earth that formed the plateau.

So back along a railway cutting and over the spongy green open (quite safe there) to lunch at the gunners' H.Q.

LETTER 42

Corps H.Q.,
25.5.1917.

I HAD a curious experience a day or two ago
in revisiting my early haunts of December,
1914.

I took the Ford car which is allotted to
me (and a very good one too) and started
off early. I went through Armentières
(which I had never seen before except in
the distance) towards our village of 1914.
I stopped the car at a place a mile or so
short of it and walked on.

You may remember my describing the
billet my company used to go back to between the village and the trenches—an old
farmhouse, with the old farmer and his
wife and Marie, a pretty girl of 17. Even
then a shell had blown away a bit of one of
the outhouses, and I didn't much expect to
find them now 2½ years later. The village

itself, I knew, had been blown to bits in the meantime. However I walked in that direction. It was a jolly day. The country looked much more cheerful in its spring green than when I knew it, sodden and bare. I got to the road where the billet was and came upon a field absolutely torn up with shell-holes, with the ruins of a farm near. Apparently the Boche had been strafing some horse lines there, and not long ago either. At first I thought the ruins were my farm, but there were no remains of the large shrine I remembered at the cross-roads. I walked on ; and 300 yards further on the shrine and billet hove in sight. After what I had just seen I felt more certain than ever there would be no one there.

I passed my old room looking out on the road (how well I remembered it—I could almost feel the snow and rain) and walked into the house. Curtains in the windows had rather surprised me. The place seemed occupied. I turned into the kitchen.

The sensation of a jump-back in time grew stronger and stronger. The kitchen was just as it used to be—a large pot on the fire, the

long settle under the window with the table
before it. A woman I did not know was
sitting working at another window —a nice-
looking woman of about 30. She rose as I
came in, and I concluded another set of
people had taken the house. Then I began
to spot a likeness to the girl ot 1914. " Êtes
vous Marie ? " I asked. She looked puzzled.
" Mariée ? " she said. " Non," I said,
" Marie — vous." " Oh," said she, " le
capitaine des Ouest-lands." It was Marie,
grave, good-looking, about ten years older.
They had stayed in the farm all this time,
in spite of the shelling all round, and worked
the land and kept their cows. Only a week
before the Boche had strafed some battery
positions in the paddock, 100 yards from the
house. There were no guns there, but the
positions were knocked to bits. The farm
had never been hit again, by wonderful luck.
I asked where they went when the shelling
was on, and Marie said " Oh, into the
cellar —or the kitchen," as one might talk
of coming in out of the rain.

   She was very ready to talk of the " Ouest-
lands," and remembered people in a very
Q 2

friendly way. I sat in the kitchen and had a glass of beer, and we had a long talk. Her father came in half-way through ; at first he didn't recognize me, and then said, " Ah yes—your brother was at Bailleul and came to see you."

The mother was away in Armentières with the son, returned on leave from Salonika, home for the first time for nearly three years.

I was very much touched by their cordiality. We were the first people to be billeted on them, and since then they had mostly had Artillery. We sat and chatted about the people of those early days. Marie Louise, a friend whom you may remember, was now in Paris. Her brother had been killed. The curé of the village had gone, as he had no church : it meant a long trudge now to Mass. I was glad to hear that no one else had succeeded in making the fireplace in the next room draw, which we had had to give up so ignominiously. A girl came in while we were talking, from the billet down the road where C Company and its commander used to be. Yes, she remembered him perfectly, the officer with the eyeglass.

I cannot tell you how strange it was,
sitting there as if 2½ years had been wiped
out, and one was back as a beginner in
France. So much, so very much has happened in that time ; and yet, in the curious
way memories revive, it seemed only a week
or two since I left the place. And with one
was of course very strongly the thought of
all those companions and friends of those
days who have gone across. A. of the eyeglass, sweet-tempered and friendly ; B.,
who came out with me, capable and ener-
getic ; C., my subaltern ; D., even in those
days already wounded in Ypres ; E., the
cheery, the last to go ; my company
Sergeant-Major, very young (all the old
N.C.O.'s had already been knocked out at
Ypres) but willing.

Of the officers whom I knew well only two
are left. There may be one or two of the
other officers.

I left the billet and walked through the
village. The last time I went along that
road, full of trench fever (for which I may be
truly grateful) seemed as yesterday. But
the village was untouched then : now it is
a ruin, and the church a mere shell.

I walked round other well-known spots, and found them full of company ; not that there was anyone to be seen. I went past the house in the Rue Delpierre, where C and D Companies used to share a Mess when we were further back. We used to come there, caked in mud, direct from the trenches.

And so back to the car and home.

LETTER 43

You will have gathered that big things were preparing in these parts. You now know from the papers that they came off on the 7th.*

The starting hour was 3.10 a.m. ; and my job was back here. I was up at half-past two. Nothing would come in for a bit, so I walked up the road. A little way out of the village it tops a rise, and from here I could see the horizon behind which lay our front of attack.

It was very strange and very tense. I had never seen a battle from so far off before : it was like looking through the wrong end of a telescope. And then one thought of all those crowded trenches, full of men and boys silently waiting for the signal, longing

* The Battle of Messines.

by that time for it to come. As I said, even back there it was very tense.

It was the end of an exquisite summer night. There was an almost full moon behind one, a little cloudy. The stars were paling, and to the left of our front the sky was growing light. It was a very peaceful half-lit scene—grey stretches of field, black masses of wood. There was the wonderful fresh smell of a summer dawn on a gentle breeze. There was some sound of firing, but not much. The impression was stillness. A cock crowed somewhere. Frogs croaked in a pond near. On the horizon, the white stars of the German Verey lights lobbed lazily up as usual and flickered down again. That was all good—he had not spotted our concentration during the night. Five minutes yet. A whirring behind, and a great black shape sailed by under the moon. It was the first contact aeroplane going out to battle. Then another and another, like great bats against the pale stars. The Verey lights still shot up and floated down, occasional and unsuspecting ; the first bird sounded a note or two : and then——

Then Hell broke loose. With a muffled
rumbling crash the guns opened in unheard-
of numbers—not absolutely simultaneously,
but growing quickly into one tremendous
throbbing roar. The whole horizon became
a mass of darting red rockets as the Boche
called frantically for help. And, half-right,
a stupendous thing happened. A vast shape
of lurid fire grew from the horizon and un-
folded itself till it seemed to stand for a
second, a solid bowl-shaped expanding thing
of flame. The earth shook—it was one of
the big mines. Then the flame died down;
and after that the flashes of the guns re-
vealed, towering higher and higher, the
great mountain of smoke it had caused. The
flashes were incessant, and played backwards
and forwards across the horizon like some
giant's fingers doing a *tour de force* on a great
keyboard.

- I stood watching the opening of this
terrific drama with bared head. Then I
turned back to the office. The daylight was
rapidly broadening and the bird-chorus growing. The office looked out into a pleasant
garden; the potato-bed and the walk be-

tween fruit trees was soon bright in the sunlight. The village woke up. The hundred or so cheerful little girls who, with the nuns who teach and manage them, share these Headquarters, began to be in evidence as one passed through the court. There were only the wires that came through to remind one that, a few miles on, our men were sweating, stabbing, falling, pressing on, facing, daring, holding, winning—for us.

LETTER 44

12th November, 1918.

To-DAY I came up on my way to London through the same country that I went down through in August, 'fourteen. Fields and woods were again lit by a low sun ; the trees, where they had any leaves, were this time clothed in brown. I thought it all very exquisite; but, instead of stirring one with the appeal of something beautiful, greatly loved, and threatened, its quiet loveliness had the quality of a caress that means (however little deserved) reward.

THE END

www.ingramcontent.com/pod-product-compliance
Lightning Source LLC
Chambersburg PA
CBHW030406100426
42812CB00028B/2851/J